The Great Life Cookbook

Whole Food, Vegan, Gluten-Free Meals for Large Gatherings

by Priscilla Timberlake & Lewis Freedman, RD

Introduction: Mark Hyman, MD • **The Apprentice's Guide:** Alicia Freedman

Photos: Alicia Freedman, Raina Timberlake-Freedman, Julie Manners, Bruce Monger and Lewis Freedman • **Book Design:** Julie Manners

Coddington Valley Publishing

2161 Coddington Road, Brooktondale, NY 14817 • info@CoddingtonValleyPublishing.com

Book Design: Julie Manners

Publication Management: Mancuso Associates Inc, Geneva, New York, USA

Printed by Worzalla Book Manufacturing in Stevens Point, Wisconsin, USA
Worzalla is a 100% employee-owned company.

Disclaimer: The recipes and dietary recommendations in this book should not be used as medical
treatment for any disease or illness. Individuals making dietary choices are responsible for their own
health and should consult their medical practitioner before undertaking any significant changes.

 **This book is printed on 100% recycled paper.**

The text is printed on Mohawk Options from Mohawk Fine Papers, a 100% Recycled Paper,
with 100% Post Consumer Waste Fiber.

The cover is printed on Reincarnation Matte from New Leaf Paper, a 100% Recycled Paper
with 60% Post Consumer Waste Fiber.

Both papers are manufactured with electricity that is offset by
renewable energy certificates.

The manufacturing of this book meets the criteria for Forest
Stewardship Council™ (FSC®) Certification. FSC® certified forest
products are verified from the forest of origin through the supply
chain. The FSC® label ensures that the forest products used are from
responsibly harvestedand verified sources.

The savings below were realized for *each and every individual copy of this book* by using these
paper choices in place of virgin fiber.

• 10.93 gals. wastewater flow saved • 1.89 lbs. solid waste not generated • 7.17 oz. of oil unused
• 3.54 lbs. net greenhouse gases prevented • 7,787 BTUs energy not consumed

We Dedicate...

The Great Life Cookbook is dedicated to **Meghan Murphy,** *(right)* whose brief visit touched us deeply. Thank you Meghan for encouraging and supporting us to create this book. Although you have transitioned to a new and different journey, your spirited vision carries on.

We Pledge...

Because there are many human beings who go hungry every day, our spiritual teacher and global humanitarian, Her Holiness Sai Maa, created the **Just One Hunger Initiative**. Launched in August of 2011, Just One Hunger feeds thousands of children in the slums of India each year.

We have pledged a portion of the proceeds from your purchase of this book to fund a contribution to this organization. Your donation will provide a full meal for one child.

www.HumanityInUnity.org
www.Sai-Maa.com

Contents

A Complete List of Menus

Serve with Kukicha Twig Tea (see page 225).

All recipes can be scaled down (see page 221).

How Eating at Home Can Save Your Life

By Mark Hyman, MD

THE SLOW INSIDIOUS DISPLACEMENT of home cooked and communally shared family meals by the industrial food system has fattened our nation and weakened our family ties. *The Great Life Cookbook,* written by my oldest dearest college friends with whom I shared countless communal meals over 30 years ago, is the catalyst that can turn this tide and help Americans take back their kitchens, take back their homes and rebuild community and connection. Health happens in community.

In 1900, two percent of meals were eaten outside the home. In 2010, 50 percent were eaten away from home and one in five breakfasts is from MacDonald's. Most family meals happen about three times a week, last less than 20 minutes and are spent watching television or texting while each family member eats a different microwaved "food." More meals are eaten in the minivan than the kitchen.

Research shows that children who have regular meals with their parents do better in every way, from better grades, to healthier relationships, to staying out of trouble. Regular family dinners protect girls from bulimia, anorexia, and diet pills. Family dinners also reduce the incidence of childhood obesity. We complain of not having enough time to cook, but Americans spend more time watching cooking on the Food Network, than actually preparing their own meals.

The family dinner has been hijacked by the food industry. The transformations of the American home and meal outlined above did not happen by accident. Broccoli, peaches, almonds, kidney beans, and other whole foods don't need a food ingredient label or bar code, but for some reason these foods—the foods we co-evolved with over millennia—had to be "improved" by Food Science. As a result, the processed-food industry and

Mark Hyman, MD is a family physician and five times #1 New York Times bestselling author. He is an internationally recognized leader in functional medicine. (www.drhyman.com)

industrial agriculture has changed our diet, decade by decade, not by accident but by intention.

Common sense and scientific research lead us to the conclusion that if we want healthy bodies we must put the right raw materials in them: real; whole; local; fresh; unadulterated; unprocessed; and chemical-, hormone-, and antibiotic-free food.

That we need nutritionists and doctors to teach us how to eat is a sad reflection of the state of society. These are things our grandparents knew without thinking twice about them. What foods to eat, how to prepare them, and an understanding of why you should share them in family and community have been embedded in cultural traditions since the dawn of human society.

The sustainability of our planet, our health, and our food supply are inextricably linked. The ecology of eating—the importance of what you put on your fork—has never been more critical to our survival as a nation or as a species. The earth will survive our self-destruction. But we may not.

I believe the most important and the most powerful tool you have to change your health and the world is your fork. Imagine an experiment—let's call it a celebration: We call upon the people of the world to join together and celebrate food for one week. For one week or even one day, we all eat breakfast and dinner at home with our families or friends. For one week we all eat only real, whole, fresh food. Imagine for a moment the power of the fork to change the world. Imagine if we did something as simple as sharing meals together—guided by *The Great Life Cookbook*—how that might transform lives bringing nourishment and healing for body, mind and spirit.

The extraordinary thing is that we have the ability to move large corporations and create social change by our collective choices. We can reclaim the family dinner, reviving and renewing it. Doing so will help us learn how to find and prepare real food quickly and simply, teach our children by example how to connect, build security, safety and social skills, meal after meal, day after day, year after year.

The Inspiraton

By Priscilla Timberlake

ON A TYPICAL SATURDAY MORNING, I sip twig tea and reflect on the previous night. There is usually much to ponder, as Friday evenings are full of activity. Nearly every Friday for the last 17 years, we have hosted locally grown, macrobiotic vegan dinners in our country home in upstate New York. A feeling of deep satisfaction flows through me for having accomplished something tangible and satisfying for my family and friends. However, these dinners are more than a shared meal; they are meaningful acts of love for our community.

Many friends and guests to our dinners have asked us to write a cookbook. With the intention of offering something unique, we decided to tell a story about our Friday night meals, as well as offer large serving recipes to encourage the sharing of this wonderful plant-based cuisine.

We hope to kindle the sacredness, healing and magic that emerges when people gather to share a meal of local food that nurtures the body, mind and soul. Our intention with this book is to offer a blueprint so that others can use it to build community around nourishing macrobiotic/vegan meals.

Macrobiotics is a philosophy of life, often translated as "big" or "great life". Our wish is that your life will be enriched through using these recipes and that you will receive contentment and gratification through cooking for others.

Perhaps you landed upon this book because you want to cook a meal that everyone can enjoy. You may have a family member or friend that doesn't eat this or that. Our dinners have evolved to be as inclusive as possible, meaning they will be agreeable to most people. All meals in this book are plant-based, dairy-free, vegan, macrobiotic, and gluten-free, with oil-free options.

If you encounter unfamiliar ingredients, turn to the Apprentice's Guide at the end of this book. The guide is a compilation of kitchen conversations that took place on Fridays while we prepared dinner and were recorded by our daughter-in-law, Alicia. I invite you to try unfamiliar ingredients, as what is new today could be commonplace tomorrow. For example, growing up in the sixties in Staten Island, NY, I have no memory of coming in contact with tofu. Today, it is available everywhere.

You will find 12 full meals in the pages that follow, one for each month of the year. There are 20 to 24 servings in each recipe, unless stated otherwise. They can be cut in half to serve 10 to 12, or quartered to serve five to six people. See *Scaling Down Recipes for Smaller Quantities* on page 221. On most Fridays, we double the recipes to serve 40 or 50 guests.

The Birth of Friday Dinner

I MET LEWIS in Ithaca, New York, while he was attending Cornell University studying nutrition, and I had just graduated. Lewis lived several miles out of town in a communal house fondly referred to as "the shack." I was a frequent visitor to this magical household. I noticed that Lewis was very happy to be involved in making healthy, scrumptious food for himself and his housemates. One lovely fall day, I happened to be visiting when a fresh loaf of whole grain bread came out of the oven and, of course, it tasted delicious! When I asked Lewis about the ingredients, he recited the usual expected ingredients: whole grain flour, yeast, sea salt, and sweetener. And, then he added, "let us not forget love." My interest in more than the bread heightened. "Who was this young handsome man anyway?"

Priscilla and Lewis with their eldest son Jonah in 1982.

In 1992 with the three boys, Jonah, Arden and Tyler.

Grandpa holding Arden.

Fifteen years later, having been married for a good chunk of that time, we returned to Ithaca from a year in Atlanta, Georgia, where Lewis was enrolled in a program at Emory University to complete his certification as a Registered Dietitian. Although we were rich with new experiences, we came home, literally, broke. Lewis was doing his best to integrate this new degree into his professional life. However, we were spending significantly more money than we brought in. Homeschooling our three boys did not leave much time for me to work outside the home. I was looking for a creative way to contribute financially to the household.

Just about this same time, my 65-year-old mother, Jean, returned from a trip to Myanmar. Two Burmese sisters had invited her to their home for an informal dinner, which they prepared regularly for tourists visiting Inle Lake. The atmosphere was full of family, the food was vegetarian, and it was delicious! In exchange, the sisters asked for a donation. My mom raved about her experience at the Burmese sisters' home. She suggested that I try something like this in my own home. I thought about a heart-warming community macrobiotic dinner that I had experienced at my friend Lynn Chittick's home in Beckett, Massachusetts, so I knew this could work. In the autumn of 1995, we hosted our first Friday Dinner.

September 2009 marked the 14th birthday of Friday Dinner, and it was serendipity that brought seven peace workers from Myanmar to our dinner table. They were from the Metta Development Foundation, which facilitates recovery from civil conflict and natural disasters. Our Myanmar friends were quite surprised when I revealed to them that the inspiration for these community meals came from their precious country.

Our Healing Stories

BOTH LEWIS AND I had experienced miraculous healing after adopting a whole foods, plant-based diet. We had been dairy-free vegetarians for years, but were not savvy about whole foods.

My healing occurred when our boys, Arden, Tyler and Jonah, were three, seven and ten. At the time, we also had my grandfather Bill Beckman living with us, whom we had kidnapped from a nursing home a few years prior. With a full house, I was taking care of everyone but myself. I was exhausted and run-down, which led to a physical break down. In addition to constant stomach cramps, my eyes, nose, and mouth were cracking and bleeding. It was as if the mucous membranes in my body were rebelling. It was a perfect time to get out my floppy hat and dark sunglasses, as I looked absolutely awful.

(above) *Tyler, Priscilla, Lewis, Raina, Arden, Jonah and Alicia in 2008.*

Courtesy of Michio and Aveline Kushi

Peace begins at home

" Peace does not begin with any political party, religious movement, or social platform. It begins in kitchens and pantries, gardens and backyards, where the physical source of our daily life — food, the staff of life, our daily bread — is grown and prepared. From individual hearts and homes, peace radiates out to friends and neighbors, communities and nations. Whoever takes charge of the cooking is our general, our pilot. Brown rice, miso soup, whole grain bread, fresh vegetables — these and other whole unprocessed foods are our weapons; to turn around the entire world. "

—Michio Kushi

I knew that the solution was to change my diet. I read about macrobiotics, and this philosophy of balance deeply resonated within me. Thanks to friends, Betty and Joel, who were brave enough to stay with our brood for 20 hours, we headed to Vermont to the Kushi Summer Camp. We went to meet with the macrobiotic teacher, healer and master himself, Micho Kushi. In a roomful of people, Mr. Kushi needed no more than 10 minutes to personally offer me his wisdom. He summed it up with, "Too yin!" I had already visited a conventional doctor, a homeopath and other healers. However, it was Kushi's two words about my condition that stirred into motion the shift in my diet which brought me back to balance and health.

As creatures in this amazing universe, we are learning how to walk in balance between yin and yang. According to the macrobiotic view, yin refers to the more expansive, outward expression of energy. Yang is the more contracted form of energy. With my severe yin condition, my sweet imbalanced blood was quite acidic. I was an ideal host for the overgrowth of the natural occurring yeast, *Candida Albicans,* which normally lives in symbiosis in the human body with other microorganisms. I was prescribed the standard healing diet of brown rice, local seasonal vegetables, beans and mineral-rich sea vegetables. Within two months, I was physically healthier than I had ever been in my life. Embracing the macrobiotic principal of eating in harmony with nature became a way of life.

Lewis also came back to health through changing his diet. As a child, his family owned a business, Freedman's Bakery, and made delicious fresh bread a staple at every meal. He worked in his family's bakery, and in the university bakery at Cornell. The cumulative effect of all those years of ingesting flour and yeast products left Lewis weakened. In his early 20's, Lewis experienced frequent intestinal pains. At times, they were so uncomfortable that he had to rest and focus on breathing through the pain. Lewis was simultaneously suffering from the pre-diabetic symptoms of hypoglycemia. It became clear that there was a direct relationship between what he was eating and how he was feeling. Through focusing on whole foods, Lewis was able to turn these conditions around and gain strength, which he has maintained to this day.

These personal health transformations add to our excitement in sharing healthy, enlivening, meals. We are grateful for our healthy bodies and have come to realize that we are ultimately responsible for caring for them.

Incidentally, Grandpa Bill lived more than seven years with us, before dying peacefully in his sleep at age 91. Pressure-cooked brown rice became a favorite of his.

More on Health, Healing and Balancing Food Combining

ON THIS NEW PATH TO HEALTH, I spent the next few years learning all I could about food and healing. I was studying macrobiotics and became thoroughly familiar with Aveline Kushi's, *Complete Guide to Macrobiotic Cooking*. Thanks to Annemarie Colbin's book, *The Natural Gourmet*, I was introduced to the fascinating Five Phase Theory of Food Combining.

Crossing over oceans and centuries, this theory is derived from the Five Element Theory in ancient Chinese Medicine. This philosophy deepened my understanding of the workings of yin and yang. As energy moves from expansive (yin) to contractive (yang) and around again, it goes through transformations.

These energy states are expressed in this theory. As we all know, energy cannot be created or destroyed. It only changes form. Seasons are good examples: cycling between the stored energy state of deep winter, to the expansive growth spurt of spring, to the explosion of summer, to the settling energy of early fall, to the contracting energy of late fall, and back to winter again.

With this theory, the five seasons correspond to five elements, which are associated with specific organs, emotions and other facets of human life. Each season/element has a matching color and taste with respect to food. Early fall is the yellow-orange earth element with a sweet taste. Late fall is white metal with a pungent taste. Winter is water with the color blue-black and a salty taste. Spring is green, associated with the wood element and the sour taste. Summer is linked with the color red, the fire element, and a bitter taste.

According to this system, a healthy balanced meal would include food from each of these elements with, perhaps, a small percentage more of those foods corresponding to the present season. We use this theory while menu planning. We look for a rainbow of color reflected back to us on the plate, and we expect the five tastes to be represented in each meal. We believe that this is another reason why our dinner guests finish their meals feeling balanced, satisfied and complete, a true experience of the "great life."

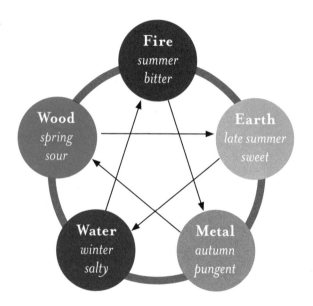

(above) *The Five Element Theory of Chinese Medicine*

(right) *Two dishes from the November menu: Green Dinosaur and Red Russian Kale with Orange Black Sesame Dressing (see page 188); and Steamed Turnips, Daikon and Carrots with Dulse (see page 181).*

Embracing Community

COOKING FOR FRIENDS is not as scary as you might think! It does not take a professional chef to put together a healthy meal for a group of people. When cooking for a crowd, all you need is intention, time, ingredients, a few large pots and pans, and a cooking space you feel good spending time in!

Providing a safe, cozy, intimate place for people to relax and to enjoy healthy food is a worthy and rewarding endeavor. At our dinners, guests sit at communal tables and enjoy each other's company.

Priscilla and Lewis

They can catch up on local news and solicit advice. Children scurry off to the playroom to find their favorite toys. Our devoted dog, Angel, is a beacon of love and affection to all; whereas our new six-toed kitten, Pepper, is a total rascal. Our two bunnies, Daisy and Chip, hop around the yard, surprising many people with their presence.

We serve the entire meal. We start with soup, then, a main plate of 5 or 6 dishes, and end with dessert. With some questioning, as well as my knack for remembering birthdays, we find one or more guests to sing *Happy Birthday* to each week.

Life is not always easy and sometimes we go through difficult times. The common practice of gathering together for meals can have a transformational effect on a person. There is something that happens energetically when people come together with the intention of promoting health and happiness. The very common air becomes charged with goodness. How healing it is to be in the presence of others, reminding us of our essential wholeness!

Raina with Angel and Pepper.

Arden in the garden.

Tyler in Paris.

Alicia & Jonah on their wedding day.

Hidden Values

I OFTEN GET ASKED THE QUESTION, "How can you spend hours cooking a meal that takes just minutes to eat? What is the sense of that?" This question sends my mind floating back to a time when a group of Tibetan Buddhist monks were invited to the Cornell campus to create a sacred sand mandala.

The monastery in Ithaca was preparing for a visit from His Holiness the Dalai Lama, and the public was invited to observe. It was quite an experience, watching these monks focus. They used special tools and containers of colored sand to slowly create a large, meaningful image. While the monks worked, the atmosphere was tranquil. After weeks of working on this majestic piece of art, the monks scooped it up into in a vessel, transforming it back to sand, and released their creation into Bebe Lake. What a lesson in impermanence! We were told that the monks' sole objective was to cultivate a pure motivation to benefit others. You can probably sense where I'm going with this. Offering healthy, delicious food is a very practical way to benefit others.

In addition to nurturing others, cooking with mindfulness fosters one's own inner peace and joy. The author of *Full Catastrophe Living*, Jon Kabat-Zinn, shares that "Mindfulness means paying attention in a particular way; on purpose, in the present moment, nonjudgementally." What a relief it is to simply focus on cooking.

This past fall, Alicia and I trekked down to New York City, to the Manhattan Center Hammerstein Ballroom on West 34th Street to spend a day of mindfulness with Thich Nhat Hanh, the venerable Zen Buddhist Vietnamese master and visionary. Along with 1,000 other participants, we ate lunch, mindfully chewing each bite 30 times as instructed. We were invited to meditate on all the beings who put time and care into getting us this precious food, including the farmer, the trucker, the cook, etc. I believe it is this kind of awareness that is the foundation for the "great life." It was quite a validation to find out that Thich Nhat Hanh, and all his monks and nuns, eat a whole food, plant-based vegan diet!

There is an artistic, creative side of cooking. Working with colorful vegetables with amazing intricate design patterns is a sensory delight. Have you ever looked closely at the cross section of a carrot or radish? It is miraculous that something so seemingly simple is, in essence, quite intricate and beautifully organized. I find inspiration and happiness in just being able to work so intimately with these lovely plant-foods.

Full Circle

RETURNING TO PRESENT TIME with our unfolding story has me sitting in front of my computer on a snowy January evening in 2012. Our wonderful 13-year-old daughter, Raina, started her life's journey here in our home. Another family member who has arrived since the conception of Friday Dinner is Alicia, our oldest son's wife. Her contribution to this book and to our lives is beyond measure.

Lewis and I are, indeed, very fortunate, living this great life within the circle of our parents and families, our wonderful children, a conscious caring community and our guides and teachers. Thank you so much for taking the time to read these musings. May this book bring you much joy and happiness, and may you share these blessings with your friends and community. *Viva the great life!*

Let the **Rainbow** Be Thy **Medicine**

By Lewis Freedman, RD

"Each day, eat from all parts of the plant, and every color of the rainbow, and you will be just fine." This is the first nutritional advice that truly resonated with me. I received these words of wisdom over 25 years ago as I talked informally with an MD about giving nutritional advice. This was the counsel he gave to his patients. He was ahead of the times and yet in line with the longest standing medical advice offered by Hippocrates in 400 B.C. "Let food be thy medicine…"

About that time, I became aware of the work of Dr. Dean Ornish. He had recently published his book, *Stress, Diet, and Your Heart,* which showed that heart disease could be reversed though a whole food, low-fat, plant-based diet, together with regular exercise and stress reduction practices including yoga, and the love of a supportive group. We all accept that daily exercise, including practices such as yoga, can be relaxing and indeed very helpful; yet it still is not enough. It is the other two aspects of his program, nutrition and community, that this cookbook addresses.

The food part is easy. Dr. T. Colin Campbell has demonstrated the validity of the science of food as medicine in a vast human study, and through extensive experiments in the lab. In a book on this subject, *The China Study,* co-authored with his son, Thomas Campbell, the facts are laid out clearly. Eating a whole food, plant-based diet will significantly reduce one's chances of developing the majority of diseases prevalent in the modern western world, including heart disease, cancer, stroke, diabetes, alzheimer's, multiple sclerosis, rheumatoid arthritis, and kidney stones, among others.

The nutrients available through eating whole foods are markedly increased as compared to those of processed foods. Through the refining process, nutrients are stripped out of foods. Compare white rice to brown rice. Brown rice has fiber as well as B-vitamins, trace minerals, and all the associated nutrients that are absent from refined white rice. Think about the life force, color, and vitality in a freshly picked green bean, versus what we see and feel when opening a can of green beans. Intuitively, we know that "whole food" refers also to the quality, freshness, and life force of the food itself!

You may have noticed that the recipes in this book contain no gluten. I believe that gluten intolerance and celiac disease are symptoms of our modern processed diet. With these problems becoming more widespread, we started to have increasingly frequent requests from guests to prepare gluten-free options. With our intention to be as inclusive as possible, we began cooking, baking and preparing the entire meal without any gluten. It is not very difficult; we buy wheat-free tamari and gluten-free oats. We make baked goods with brown rice flour and oat flour, and we use brown rice noodles. The reward is the smiles of gratitude on the faces of guests who usually "can't eat anything." Here, they can enjoy the full meal.

Another point of inclusiveness is the option of preparing each dish without added oil. In his book, *Prevent and Reverse Heart Disease,* Dr. Caldwell Esselstyn, Jr. has clearly shown that the findings of Dr. Ornish are valid and consistently reproducible, and that with a low-fat, whole food, plant-based, and no-added oil diet, heart disease can be stopped and even reversed. In the macrobiotic approach, a period of oil-free cooking may be necessary to heal and rebalance the body. In this light, most of our recipes do not include added oils, and for those that do, an oil-free option is provided.

This brings me to the point of looking more closely at what nutrition really means and how we nurture ourselves. I have already mentioned the strong evidence for eating a whole food, plant-based diet. So, what more is there? As Dr. Ornish demonstrated, having a social network—a loving embrace from your community—is fundamental to good health. It is now accepted that social support is a key element in the quality of life, and even of longevity. Sharing a healthy meal indeed nurtures the body, and it does so much more. The conversation and camaraderie of a loving community also deeply nourishes the spirit.

Joining together with friends and family to share a health-supporting meal is indeed vital to living *The Great Life.*

(right) *A full plate from the December menu. See pages 163-177 for recipes.*

Dinners by the Month

Twelve Complete Meals from Soup to Dessert

January

(left) *Arame, Leeks and Tempeh with Sunflower Seeds;* (above) *Collard Rolls, with collard filling*

Green Split Pea and Navy Bean Soup

Prep Notes: Prepare vegetables after starting to cook split peas.
A large 8 quart pot is needed.

2 cups dried navy beans
4 cups dried green split peas
1 four-inch strip of kombu or kelp
3 quarts water
6 medium carrots, diced small (~3 cups)
2 medium yellow onions, diced small (~2½ cups)
2 medium red onions, diced small (~2½ cups)
1 teaspoon sea salt
8 celery stalks, diced small
4 tablespoons wheat-free or regular tamari
1 bunch parsley, chopped for garnish

1. Soak navy beans and kombu or kelp in 1 quart of water, overnight or 8 hours.

2. Rinse beans after soaking. In a pressure cooker, add beans, sea vegetable that was soaked with beans, and 4 cups of fresh water. Bring to a boil, uncovered. Skim off foam and, when the foaming stops, lock lid into place. Bring to pressure and cook on low heat for one hour or less depending on the amount of pounds of pressure in your cooker. If boiling instead of pressure cooking, cook for 1½ hours.

3. Bring split peas and 8 cups of water to a boil in a large pot. Lower heat, cover, and let simmer for approximately 1½ hours.

4. Add onions and carrots to split peas and cook for 5 minutes.

5. Add cooked navy beans with cooking liquid, chopped sea vegetable and salt to split pea pot and simmer for 10 minutes.

6. Add celery and tamari to split pea pot and simmer for 10 minutes more.

7. Garnish with parsley.

Fluffy Kasha with Miso Tahini Sauce

PREP NOTES: A large cast iron pan works best for this. Kasha is also called buckwheat groats. This warming winter grain is from the rhubarb family and is simple to prepare. A small amount of steam needs to be released as the kasha is cooking. This helps to achieve a fluffy consistency.

    4 cups buckwheat groats
    8 cups water
    1½ teaspoons sea salt

1. In a large pot, bring water and salt to boil.

2. Rinse buckwheat and dry-roast in a pan for several minutes, until fragrant. Use a wooden spoon and stir to keep from burning.

3. Add boiling water to roasted kasha.

4. Lower to simmer, cover with lid slightly ajar, and cook for 20 to 25 minutes.

5. Let sit a few minutes and fluff with a fork.

Miso Tahini Sauce

    ½ cup sesame tahini
    2 tablespoons sweet white miso
    ½ cup water

1. Mix all ingredients together with a fork or whisk until smooth.

2. Place a heaping teaspoon of sauce on each serving of kasha.

Steamed Rutabagas, Parsnips and Carrots with Toasted Hazelnuts

PREP NOTES: Freshly shelled hazelnuts are best. The toasting of the nuts brings out the flavor. If the root vegetables are smooth and clean, there is no need to peel. If dirty and wrinkly, wash, peel and cut off the unappealing sections. Be aware that the rutabagas may be waxed, and if so, definitely peel.

> 1 cup raw hazelnuts
> 3 medium rutabagas (~6 cups)
> 6 medium parsnips (~4 cups)
> 6 medium carrots (~4 cups)

1. Toast hazelnuts on a baking sheet in oven for 10 to 12 minutes at 350 degrees. Turn once or twice so they do not burn. Allow nuts to cool for a few minutes and then chop coarsely.

2. Wash root vegetables well. Cut into large chunks, 1 to 2 inches thick. Keep the rutabagas, parsnips and carrots separated. In a large steamer; keep each in their own section. A layered steamer would also work well.

3. Steam the vegetables until they are tender. The different vegetables will vary in cooking time.

4. Toss all together with roasted hazelnuts and serve.

Pressed Medley Salad with Tangerine Dressing

PREP NOTES: The green apples add a nice sweet and tart touch.

> 1 large head green cabbage
> 1 bunch red radishes
> 2 green apples
> 6 stalks celery
> 1 tablespoon sea salt
> 6 tangerines
> 2 teaspoons brown rice vinegar

1. Slice cabbage into long thin strips.

2. Chop radishes and apples into thin matchstick shaped pieces.

3. Thinly slice celery crosswise.

4. Using your hands mix salt in thoroughly with all the ingredients except for tangerines and rice vinegar.

5. Press in a large bowl. A ceramic bowl with steep edges works best. Place a plate on top, one that is just slightly smaller than the diameter of the bowl. Place a weight on top. A glass gallon jug full of water, works great. *(See photo on page 69.)* Press for 4 or more hours.

6. In a separate bowl, mix the rice vinegar with the juice of the tangerines.

7. When it is time to serve your guests, remove the weight and rinse the salt off of the vegetables. Drain well. Toss the pressed vegetables with the tangerine vinegar dressing.

Arame, Leeks and Tempeh with Sunflower Seeds

PREP NOTES: Soak arame, a sea vegetable, for 1 hour or more. A large pan is needed. To make this without oil, toss the sliced tempeh with 2 tablespoons of tamari and broil on a baking sheet until browned on all sides. *See photo on page 28.*

> 3 packed cups dry arame, soaked for 1 hour in 3 cups water
> 6 to 8 medium leeks
> 1 pound soy tempeh
> ½ cup raw sunflower seeds
> 6 cloves garlic, minced
> 2 tablespoons fresh ginger root, minced or finely grated
> 1 tablespoon toasted sesame oil *(optional)*
> 2 tablespoons mirin (rice cooking wine)
> 5 tablespoons wheat-free or regular tamari

1. Strain the arame, saving the liquid.

2. Prepare leeks by cutting them entirely in half lengthwise and cleaning well under running water. Pay particular attention to the point where the leeks emerged from the ground and soil entered into the leek's leaf folds. *See photo page 100.* Slice the leeks horizontally in ¼ inch thick half circles. Separate the top dark green parts from the white bottoms, keeping both sections.

3. Slice tempeh into thin rectangles, approximately 1 inch by ½ inch by ¼ inch thick. Sauté in sesame oil until browned on both sides. Set aside. *See Prep Notes for oil-free instructions.*

4. Toast sunflower seeds in a hot dry skillet, stirring constantly.

5. Sauté the white leek sections, garlic and ginger in water for 5 minutes in a large pan at medium heat. When water sautéing, have a cup of water nearby and add small amounts of water as needed.

6. Fold in greens of leeks and tempeh. Simmer for 10 to 12 minutes.

7. Add toasted sunflower seeds and 3 more tablespoons of tamari. Stir gently for 1 minute and serve.

Collard Rolls

PREP NOTES: Make sure to drain water off of collards after blanching, or the rolls will turn out soggy. This is a great green dish that can be prepared ahead of time. It is wonderful for parties. For a complete green roll, use only collards. *See photo on page 29.*

> 24 large collard leaves
> Several tablespoons of umeboshi plum vinegar
> 2 medium carrots
> ½ small red cabbage

1. Cut the stems off the collards at the base of the leaves.

2. Bring a large pot, half filled with water, to a boil. Boil small batches of collard leaves for about 2 minutes, until bright green. Be careful not to overcook because the leaves will tear easily. Remove and cool immediately with cold water to stop the cooking,

3. Drain collards well. Lay them out on a clean dry towel and pat dry.

4. Cut carrots in long thin slivers and blanch for a minute, until bright orange. Cool immediately in cold water.

5. Cut red cabbage in long thin slivers and blanch for 2 minutes. Cool thoroughly in cold water.

6. Line 4 collard leaves up on top of each other with the insides facing up, and every other layer facing in an opposite direction (top to bottom, bottom to top).

7. Sprinkle a touch of umeboshi vinegar on each leaf as you stack them.

8. Place a thin row of carrots and cabbage across the center of the collards.

9. Starting from one of the long sides, roll tightly. Do your best to get the carrots and red cabbage centered in the roll. Slice into bite-sized sections when ready to serve. A serrated blade works well. Serve at room temperature.

Sweet Potato Fries

PREP NOTES: Jewel and garnet are the sweet potato varieties most commonly sold where we live; they are sometimes labeled as yams. Wash them well and do not peel. These fries are also delicious when made without oil, simply replace the oil with twice the amount of water.

16 medium sweet potatoes
2 tablespoons olive oil *(optional)*
Sea salt
Black pepper

1. Cut sweet potatoes in long ½ inch by 1 inch thick strips or wedges.

2. Place in large bowl and toss with olive oil, or water.

3. Distribute the sweet potatoes on three lightly-oiled baking pans. Bake at 375 degrees for 1 to 1½ hours, turning every so often.

4. Remove from heat. Sprinkle with sea salt and a dash of black pepper. Serve hot.

I have been coming to the Friday Night Dinner since the first one, 17 years ago. I am still always surprised by the quality and creativity of the meal.

—**Martin Kelly-Smyth**
Energy Kinesiologist

Key Lime Parfait

PREP NOTES: Each step involves cooling and gelling, so allow for plenty of time. You will need 3 medium sized bowls. This recipe makes 22 to 24 parfait glasses, small bowls or cups, of at least 6 ounces each. It is possible to substitute agar powder for the flakes, at ¼ the volume. If using the powder, whisk longer and thoroughly to avoid clumping. When assembling an ingredient list, notice that the following are used more than once in this recipe: soymilk, agar-agar, brown rice syrup, maple syrup and vanilla.

Soymilk Kanten for Topping

1 quart unsweetened vanilla soymilk

5 tablespoons agar-agar flakes

1. In a saucepan bring soymilk to a boil, whisk in flakes and boil until flakes are dissolved.

2. Set aside to firm for at least 1½ hours, preferably in a cold place.

Bottom Pudding Layer

9 limes (~1½ cups juice)

1 quart unsweetened soymilk

1 quart apple juice

2 cups brown rice syrup

1 cup pure maple syrup

1 teaspoon sea salt

1 tablespoon vanilla extract

10 tablespoons agar-agar flakes

5 tablespoons arrowroot

1. Remove zest from limes with a zester or fine grater and set aside.

2. Juice the limes.

3. Whisk all the ingredients together, except the agar-agar flakes, arrowroot, ½ cup soymilk and lime zest.

4. Transfer this mixture to a pot, add agar-agar flakes, and bring to a boil, making sure the agar-agar flakes dissolve.

5. Dissolve the arrowroot in the reserved ½ cup soymilk.

6. Whisk arrowroot mixture into the pot and simmer for 5 minutes.

7. Stir ⅔ of the lime zest into the pot.

8. Remove from heat and let cool.

9. While still warm, remove 2½ cups of the gelled pudding mixture and pour into a bowl to save for the top layer.

10. Take the remaining pudding mixture and pour into 6 ounce parfait glasses, small bowls or cups. Fill the bowls about half way.

Topping

16 ounces soft tofu
Soymilk kanten from first step
2½ cups gelled lime pudding from second step
1 cup pure maple syrup
1 cup brown rice syrup
Pinch of sea salt
2 teaspoons vanilla extract

1. Place the tofu in small pot with enough water to cover.

2. Boil the tofu for ten minutes; rinse in cold water and drain thoroughly.

3. In a blender, blend together the tofu, soymilk kanten, gelled lime pudding, rice syrup, maple syrup, vanilla and sea salt to create the smooth topping for the dessert. This may take several minutes to get the desired smooth consistency.

4. Spoon the topping onto the gelled bottom layer.

5. Lastly, use the remaining lime zest to garnish.

6. Refrigerate for at least an hour before serving.

February

(left) *Priscilla preparing Baked Root Vegetables.* (above) *Red Heart Daikon Pickles*

Macro Minestrone Soup

PREP NOTES: This soup is a meal in itself, and serves at least 24 people. The kidney beans and chickpeas will each need to soak for at least 8 hours. Then cook separately. An 8-quart pot will be necessary.

2 cups dried kidney beans

1 cup dried chickpeas

2 strips kombu or kelp, each 4 inches long

3 small leeks

½ pound small rice noodles

1 medium yellow onion, diced small (~1¼ cups)

8 cloves garlic, minced

2 tablespoons dried basil

1 tablespoon dried oregano

6 medium carrots, diced small (~3 cups)

4 quarts water

1 small head cauliflower, separated into small pieces (~3 cups)

2 teaspoons sea salt

2 tablespoons mirin or rice cooking wine

¾ cup brown rice syrup

2 tablespoons balsamic vinegar

3 tablespoons wheat-free or regular tamari

Pinch of black pepper

6 stalks celery, including the leafy tops, diced small

3 tablespoons dark brown rice miso

1. Rinse and then soak the chickpeas in 4 cups of water with a strip of kombu or kelp. Use a container with enough room for the beans to expand. Rinse and then soak the kidney beans in another container in 2 cups of water with one strip of kombu or kelp. Let both batches of beans sit and soak for at least 8 hours or overnight.

2. With both types of beans, discard soaking water and replace with fresh water to cover the beans by 1 to 2 inches; include the same piece of sea vegetable used for soaking.

3. Bring the chickpeas to a boil and skim off the foam. When the foam tapers off, place the lid on pressure cooker and bring up to pressure. Then turn the flame down, maintaining pressure and cook for 1 hour or less depending on pounds of pressure in your cooker. If cooking the beans in a regular pot with a lid, it will take an extra half hour.

4. To cook the kidney beans, follow the directions for the chickpeas, but for only 45 minutes in a pressure cooker.

5. Prepare leeks by cutting them entirely in half lengthwise and cleaning well under running water. *See photo page 100.* Separate the top dark green parts from the white bottoms, keeping both parts. Dice small.

6. Cook the noodles in a separate pot according to package directions and set aside. Be sure not to overcook. You want them al dente (slightly firm).

7. In a large pot, water sauté the onions, bottoms of leeks, garlic, basil and oregano for 5 minutes.

8. Add the carrots and sauté for a few more minutes.

9. Add water, cauliflower, salt, mirin, brown rice syrup, vinegar, tamari and black pepper, and cook covered for 30 minutes on medium heat.

10. Add chickpeas, kidney beans, chopped sea vegetable and simmer for 15 more minutes.

11. Add celery, noodles and green parts of leeks, and simmer for 6 to 8 minutes.

12. Dissolve rice miso in ½ cup of the soup broth and return to pot. Simmer for a couple minutes and serve.

Corn Muffins

PREP NOTES: This recipe makes 2 dozen. These muffins are very moist, and the corn is a nice chewy addition. To make this oil-free, substitute applesauce for the apple juice and reduce soymilk to ½ cup.

2 cups corn meal

1 cup brown rice flour

1 cup gluten-free oats blended into flour

2 tablespoons baking powder

Pinch of sea salt

½ cup brown rice syrup

¼ cup pure maple syrup

1 cup unsweetened soymilk

1 cup apple juice or cider

½ cup safflower oil *(oil-free option in Prep Notes)*

8 ounces soft tofu

2 teaspoons umeboshi plum vinegar

12 ounces frozen corn, or 2 cups fresh corn

1. Preheat oven to 350 degrees.

2. Mix the dry ingredients together.

3. In a blender, mix all of the wet ingredients together, except for the vinegar and corn.

4. Oil the muffin pans.

5. Stir the wet ingredients into the dry. Stir in vinegar and fold in corn.

6. Quickly distribute batter into muffin pans.

7. Bake for 20 to 25 minutes.

Hiziki, Red Onions and Carrots with Anita's Peanut Sauce

PREP NOTES: Soak the hiziki for an hour and then cook for 45 minutes. Large matchstick cuts are ¼ inch by ¼ inch by 2 inches. This recipe is also good with arame sea vegetable.

1½ cups dried hiziki
3¾ cups water
1½ teaspoons wheat-free or regular tamari
6 medium carrots, cut into large matchsticks (~3 cups)
1 large yellow onion, cut in half-moon slivers
1 large red onion, cut in half-moon slivers
1 lemon, juiced

1. Soak the hiziki in water for 1 hour or more.

2. Simmer the hiziki for 45 minutes in a covered small pot. Then add tamari and turn off heat.

3. Blanch vegetables separately.

4. After blanching, sprinkle lemon juice onto the red onions to bring out the lovely pink color.

5. Fold the cooked vegetables into hiziki after it has been removed from the heat. Serve hot with Anita's Peanut Sauce.

Anita's Peanut Sauce

PREP NOTES: Delicious on steamed vegetables or noodles. Serve this sauce hot or cold.

> 10 tablespoons crunchy natural peanut butter
> 4 tablespoons mirin
> 2 tablespoons umeboshi vinegar
> 3 tablespoons wheat-free or regular tamari
> 5 tablespoons brown rice syrup
> 2 tablespoons brown rice vinegar
> 3 tablespoons water

1. Mix all of the ingredients together until smooth.

2. Heat the sauce on a low flame and spoon onto each serving of hiziki and vegetables.

When I attend Friday Dinners, I am transported to a strong and joyous feeling of connection. I am reminded of the way I felt in my great grandmother's kitchen.

—**Anita Devine**
Therapist and Macrobiotic Chef

Broccoli and Kale with Green Goddess Dressing

4 medium heads broccoli, including stalks
4 bunches kale

1. Cut broccoli into large bite-sized pieces, including the softer light green insides of the broccoli stems. Remove the harder outside layer of the stems.

2. Pull leaves off kale stems. Chop stems of kale into bite-sized pieces. Chop leaves into larger bite-sized pieces.

3. Blanch stems of broccoli until tender, and then blanch large bite-sized flower tops for just a few minutes, until bright green.

4. Blanch chopped kale stems until green and soft enough to chew. Lastly, blanch the kale leaves, which will not take as long as the stems.

5. Mix vegetables together and serve, topped with Green Goddess Dressing.

Green Goddess Dressing

PREP NOTES: To make an oil-free dressing, blend one head of lettuce instead of the oil.

> 2 cups parsley (~1½ bunches)
> 3 scallions
> ⅓ cup olive oil *(oil-free option in Prep Notes)*
> 3 tablespoons umeboshi plum paste
> 1 cup water

1. Discard the stems of the parsley, just below where the stems meet the leaves.

2. Cut the rooted ends off the scallions, discard.

3. In a blender, mix all ingredients until smooth.

4. Keep in refrigerator until serving.

Pressure Cooked Brown Rice

PREP NOTES: Soaking the rice for a few hours improves the texture. The rice becomes moist and chewy at the same time. Short grain brown rice is a main staple in the macrobiotic diet, as it is a very balanced food and chock full of nutrition. When pressure cooked, it is a great source of strength, energy and endurance.

> 6 cups short grain brown rice
> 7½ cups water (9 cups if boiling)
> 1 teaspoon sea salt

1. Rinse rice thoroughly with cold water. To do this, cover the rice with water, swirl with your fingers, strain off the water, and then repeat this 1 or 2 more times.

2. Place rice and fresh water in a large pressure cooker.

3. For the best results, allow rice to soak for several hours before cooking.

4. After soaking, add salt, leave lid off and start cooking at high heat.

5. When the water begins to boil, lock the pressure cooker lid into place. When it reaches pressure, reduce heat to low (just high enough to maintain pressure).

6. Cook under pressure for 45 to 50 minutes.

7. Remove from heat and allow pressure to come down on its own before opening the lid.

8. Before serving, stir gently with a wooden spoon.

Gomashio (Roasted Sesame Seed Salt)

PREP NOTES: Gomashio is nice to have around. Guests sprinkle it on everything.

  1 cup unhulled sesame seeds
  2 teaspoons sea salt

1. Wash seeds. Rinse in fine mesh colander/strainer.

2. Roast on medium heat in a heavy-bottomed pan, stirring constantly for 10 to 15 minutes.

3. When the seeds turn a darker brown, are fragrant, and can be crushed between your fingers, pour them into a suribachi (ceramic bowl with ridges). *See photo on page 223.*

4. Roast salt quickly in same pan, add to seeds and grind in the suribachi. The seeds can also be ground in a food processor.

5. Place in a glass shaker or in a small bowl with a spoon for serving.

Baked Root Vegetables

PREP NOTES: In this dish, exact measurements of vegetables are not necessary. A large hotel pan with dimensions of 20 by 12 by 2½ inches, or its equivalent, is needed. *See photo on page 42.*

> 3 parsnips
> 3 rutabagas
> 3 turnips
> 5 medium sweet potatoes, peeled
> 2 red onions
> ½ cup brown rice syrup
> 2 tablespoons prepared mustard
> 3 tablespoons sweet white miso
> 1 teaspoon cinnamon
> ¾ cup apple juice or cider

1. Cut all the vegetables into large, but still bite-sized, chunks. Place in a large bowl.

2. Combine and whisk all other ingredients together in a small bowl. Then mix this sauce in with the vegetables.

3. Spread everything into a deep hotel pan or 2 glass baking dishes. Cover using baking sheets or foil.

4. Bake at 350 degrees for about 2 hours (possibly longer depending on how deep the vegetables are layered in the pan); stir and baste the vegetables every 30 minutes.

5. Test the vegetables by sliding a knifepoint into them. If it goes in easily, they are done.

Red Heart Daikon Pickles

PREP NOTES: Allow for several hours of pickling time. *See photo on page 43.*

3 medium or large daikon radishes
⅓ cup umeboshi plum vinegar
⅔ cup water

1. Using a vegetable peeler and a sharp knife, shape each daikon radish into a heart shape. To do this, first peel, then cut a groove lengthwise into the radish. Then, using the peeler and knife, shape the daikon into a long heart shape.

2. Slice thin, and immerse in vinegar and water.

3. Let sit for several hours.

Almond Un-Cheesecake with Blueberry Glaze

PREP NOTES: This recipe takes some time, but it is well worth it. We spent three years on this recipe, after being inspired by an almond cheesecake at the Zen Palate Restaurant in New York City. It has a great shelf life in the refrigerator, due to all the lemons. It freezes well. This cake is best made a day ahead, as its texture is developed by completely cooling before serving. Notice that the following ingredients are used more than once in this recipe: maple syrup, lemons, brown rice syrup, vanilla extract and arrowroot. This recipe makes enough for a single 10-inch springform pan (20 slices). Omit the crust if you want this dessert to be oil-free.

Crust

1 cup gluten-free or regular rolled oats
1 cup brown rice flour
¼ teaspoon sea salt
5 tablespoons pure maple syrup
5 tablespoons safflower oil

1. Heat oven to 375 degrees and oil a 10 inch springform pan.

2. Blend oats in a food processor, or blender, until almost as fine textured as flour.

3. Mix all ingredients together.

4. Spread the uncooked crust into an oiled springform pan, working the batter ¾ up the side walls. (If necessary, wet hands lightly to work the mixture.) It will be a thin layer.

5. Bake until it begins to brown (12 to 15 minutes).

6. Set aside.

Filling

2¼ cups raw almonds

4 lemons

36 ounces firm tofu

1¼ cups pure maple syrup

1½ cups brown rice syrup

½ teaspoon sea salt

1 tablespoon vanilla extract

1 tablespoon almond extract

4 tablespoons arrowroot powder

1. Remove the zest from the lemons and set the zest aside.

2. Juice the lemons (should be ¾ cup). Set juice aside.

3. Blanch and remove the skins from the almonds. To do this, bring 1 quart of water to boil, add almonds, let boil for 5 minutes, and then place almonds in cold water. Squeeze the almonds between your fingers to remove the skins. Discard the skins.

4. Mix the lemon juice and maple syrup with the almonds, and puree in a food processor or blender.

5. Mix this almond puree in a large bowl with the rest of the ingredients, except the zest and the arrowroot. It is easier if you break the tofu up with your hands first.

6. Blend until smooth. This is a key step; the smoother, the better. You can do one of the following. Use a blender, mixing in small batches. Use a food processor and a blender; first blending in the food processor, then in the blender. Or, if you have a very strong blender, you may be able to blend all in one step.

7. Before removing each batch from the blender, mix in some of the zest and some of the arrowroot.

8. Continue blending until everything is smooth and all the zest and arrowroot are mixed in.

9. Pour the batter into the crust in the springform pan; the batter may be above the top of the crust.

10. Bake at 350 degrees for approximately 1½ hours. The cake is done when it browns on the edges and the center looks baked, with cracks appearing on the top.

11. After cooling, top with Blueberry Glaze.

12. Keep cool until it is time to serve, and then gently remove outer springform. First, run a knife along the edge.

13. Slice and serve.

Blueberry Glaze

PREP NOTES: Allow an hour or more for topping to cool and gel. Agar powder may be used instead of flakes, at ¼ the volume of the flakes. If you are using powder, it is important to whisk longer and thoroughly to avoid clumping.

2 small lemons

1 cup apple juice

1 cup brown rice syrup

¼ cup pure maple syrup

3 cups blueberries (fresh or frozen)

Pinch of sea salt

4 tablespoons agar-agar flakes

2 tablespoons arrowroot powder

2 tablespoons water

1 teaspoon vanilla extract

1. Remove zest from lemons and set zest aside.

2. Juice lemons and set juice aside.

3. In a 2 quart pot, mix apple juice, brown rice syrup, maple syrup, blueberries, lemon, sea salt and agar-agar.

4. Bring to boil over medium heat. Reduce heat and simmer for a few minutes.

5. Dissolve arrowroot in 2 tablespoons of cold water.

6. Whisk arrowroot mixture into the pot and simmer for 2 more minutes.

7. Remove from heat, add lemon zest, vanilla and stir.

8. Set aside to cool.

9. Spread onto Un-Cheesecake.

March

{ 61 }

(left) *Beet and Red Onion Pickle;* (above) *Millet Almond Balls*

Curried Red Lentil Soup

PREP NOTES: Lentils are great when there is no time for an overnight soaking of beans. Red lentils cook very quickly. Green lentils are what most think of as the standard "brown" lentil. In general, lentils are easy to digest and are adaptable to different flavoring blends. A large pot, 8 quart or more, is needed.

6 cups red lentils

4 quarts water

1 medium head cauliflower (~4 cups)

2 medium yellow onions, diced small (~2½ cups)

2 tablespoons sesame oil or water

3 tablespoons cumin powder

1 tablespoon curry powder

8 medium carrots, diced small (~4 cups)

6 stalks celery with leaves, diced small

6 tablespoons wheat-free or regular tamari

2 teaspoons sea salt

1. Rinse lentils, add water and let soak for 1 hour.

2. Cook lentils in large pot at medium heat for 30 minutes.

3. Separate cauliflower into small bite-sized pieces. Set aside.

4. Sauté onions in oil, or water, for a few minutes. Add cumin and curry powders and sauté for 2 or 3 minutes longer. If onion mixture becomes too dry, stir in a few tablespoons of water.

5. Add sautéed mixture to lentils and cook for 10 minutes.

6. Add cauliflower and carrots and cook for 10 more minutes.

7. Add celery, salt, and tamari and cook for 5 to 10 minutes.

Millet Almond Balls

PREP NOTES: Folks love finger foods like these balls. It feels like a treat. This recipe makes about fifty 2 inch balls. *See photo on page 61.*

5 cups dry millet
12½ cups water
2 teaspoons sea salt
2¾ cups raw almonds
2½ tablespoons wheat-free or regular tamari
1¼ cup currants
2 cups chopped parsley (1 large bunch)

1. Rinse and drain the millet, place into a large cooking pot, add water and sea salt.

2. Bring to a boil; lower heat to simmer, cover and cook for 25 minutes.

3. In a bowl, toss almonds with tamari. Place on baking sheet and bake at 350 degrees until evenly toasted, 10 to 12 minutes. Stir every few minutes.

4. Chop almonds by hand or in a food processor, and be careful not to blend too long. We want it coarse with noticeable pieces, rather than a powder.

5. Stir 2 cups of the chopped almonds and 1 cup of currents into hot cooked millet. Leave ¾ cup of almonds and ¼ cup of currants for later.

6. When millet is cool enough to handle, mix in parsley and mold into balls, approximately 2 inches in diameter.

7. In a small bowl, mix remaining chopped almonds and currants. Lightly roll each ball in this mix.

8. Let sit for 20 minutes or more before serving.

Sautéed Gingered Greens

PREP NOTES: The ginger gives the greens a nice kick! Add more water as needed while sautéing.

3 bunches kale
1 medium head green cabbage, cut into bite-sized squares
2 medium onions, diced small (~2½ cups)
2 tablespoons fresh ginger root, finely grated or minced
¼ cup water *(more as needed)*
3 tablespoons wheat-free or regular tamari

1. Remove the kale leaves from the stems. Dice stems into small pieces. Chop leaves into large bite-sized pieces. Prepare cabbage.

2. Sauté ginger and onions in water for 5 minutes.

3. Add cabbage and cook for 3 minutes.

4. Add stems of kale and cook for a minute.

5. Add kale leaves; cook until kale is soft enough to chew and still green. This takes no more than 3 to 4 minutes.

6. Add tamari and serve.

Community meals provide a beautiful place for my family to experience the tapestry of nourishment and love through friends and food.

—Karen Keeley
mother and student of yoga
(with children Harmony, Jahya and Elijah)

Broccoli Tofu Bake

PREP NOTES: A favorite with kids of all ages. Substitute 4 cups (½ pound) fresh mushrooms for the 2 ounces dried. A large hotel pan is needed, with dimensions of 20 by 12 by 2½ inches or its equivalent. This recipe makes 24 large servings or 32 smaller.

2 ounces dried shitake mushrooms

7 medium yellow onions, diced small (~8½ cups)

2 tablespoons dried or ¼ cup fresh basil (finely chopped)

6 medium cloves garlic, minced

6-7 medium broccoli heads plus stems (~16 cups)

2 tablespoons sesame oil or water

8 pounds firm tofu

3 cups water

10 tablespoons sesame tahini

10 tablespoons umeboshi plum vinegar

3½ tablespoons umeboshi plum paste

8 ounces brown rice mochi

1. Soak shitake mushrooms in enough water to cover for 1 hour at room temperature. If using fresh mushrooms skip this step.

2. Cut broccoli tops into large bite-sized pieces. Cut or peel the tough outer skins off of the broccoli stems, and dice the softer light green inside stems.

3. Remove shitake mushroom stems, dice into small pieces and sauté with onions, basil, garlic and diced stems of broccoli in sesame oil or water.

4. With a good blender or food processor, cream together the tofu, water, tahini, umeboshi vinegar, and umeboshi paste until very smooth.

5. Blanch broccoli tops for 2 to 3 minutes and quickly cool. They will be just barely cooked.

6. Preheat the oven to 350 degrees.

7. Fold mushroom/onion mixture and blanched broccoli into blended tofu.

8. Place in large hotel pan or equivalent.

9. Grate mochi on top.

10. Bake with cover for 1 hour (aluminum foil or a baking sheet work fine).

11. Bake for 15 minutes more without cover.

Beet and Red Onion Pickles

PREP NOTES: Before boiling the beets, cut off the stems. After combining, allow a few hours for the flavors to merge and develop. *See photo with orange and yellow beets on page 60.*

> 6 large beets
> 3 large red onions
> ½ cup brown rice syrup
> 4 tablespoons brown rice vinegar
> ¼ teaspoon sea salt

1. Cover beets with water in pot. Bring to boil, reduce heat to medium and cook for 30 minutes.

2. Cut onions into half moons.

3. Blanch onions for 1 minute and then cool with cold water.

4. Move beets into cool water. Remove skins by squeezing and sliding fingers across the surface. Any difficult areas can be cut off with a knife. Then slice in large sections, ¼ to ½ inch thick.

5. Mix rice syrup, vinegar and salt together. Then add this to beets and onions. Set aside for a few hours.

Pressed Salad with Watercress and Lemon

PREP NOTES: Any lettuce mix will work. The freshness of pressed salad is a unique addition to the meal. Thin matchstick cuts are approximately the width of a wooden kitchen match.

- 1 bunch watercress, coarsely chopped
- 1 small head nappa cabbage, cut into long slivers
- 1 bunch red radishes, cut into thin matchstick pieces
- 1 pound mixed lettuce, cut into thin slices
- 2 teaspoons sea salt
- 1 lemon, juiced

1. Add sea salt to vegetables, using your hands to mix deeply. Save the lemon for later.

2. Press in a large bowl. A ceramic bowl with steep edges works best. Place a plate on top that is just slightly smaller than the diameter of the bowl. Place a weight on top. A glass gallon jug full of water works great, or use another bowl or pot filled with water. Press for 4 or more hours.

3. After pressing, rinse off the excess salt with water, drain well and mix in the juice of the lemon.

Stovetop Root Vegetables
with Pumpkin Seed Dulse

1 small buttercup squash
3 medium rutabagas
4 medium parsnips
4 medium turnips
1 three-inch strip of kombu or kelp

1. Peel squash, cut in half and remove seeds.

2. Chop all vegetables into large bite-sized chunks (~1½ inch cubes.)

3. Place kombu or kelp on the bottom of a large cast iron pan, (or 2 pans, if you only have smaller pans) adding just enough water to cover the kombu.

4. Arrange the vegetables, keeping each of the vegetables separate in their own piles, like a pie divided into sections.

5. Cover with a tight fitting lid and cook on a high flame until it boils.

6. Turn down to simmer and cook until tender, about 20 minutes. Periodically, check that there is just enough water to prevent the vegetables from burning.

7. Gently toss vegetables together. Cut sea vegetable into bite-sized pieces and stir into vegetables. Sprinkle each serving with a teaspoon of Pumpkin Seed Dulse *(recipe is on the next page)*.

Pumpkin Seed Dulse

PREP NOTES: This is a great condiment that can be sprinkled on all types of root vegetable dishes. Use the whole dulse, not the flakes. Be mindful during toasting, as both dulse and pumpkin seeds burn easily.

   1 cup raw pumpkin seeds
   1 cup dried dulse sea vegetable

1. Toast the seeds in a cast iron pan on the stovetop, or on a baking sheet in the oven at 325 degrees for 8 to 10 minutes, or until just barely browned.

2. Toast the dulse just the same as for the pumpkin seeds, being careful not to burn. The dulse should be crisp and dry so it can be ground with the seeds.

3. Combine and grind to a course consistency in a suribachi or mortar and pestle. A blender or food processor will also work, however, be careful not to overblend.

Apple Plum Bar with Orange Topping

PREP NOTES: Start by soaking the prunes in apple juice. Then make the Orange Topping. While the topping is cooling, begin with the top and bottom layers of the bar. When the bottom layer is in the oven, begin making the filling. For the topping, agar powder may be substituted for the flakes, at ¼ the volume. If using powder, whisk longer and thoroughly to avoid clumping. Apple juice, oranges, and cinnamon are used more than once in this recipe. This dessert is very rich, so pieces are cut small. Use a 9 x 12 inch baking dish.

To make this dessert oil-free, in the top and bottom layers, substitute unsweetened applesauce for the apple juice and brown rice syrup for the oil. Do not prebake the bottom layer.

Filling

1½ pounds dried pitted plums (prunes)
1 cup apple juice
4 medium apples
Pinch of sea salt
3 medium oranges (~¾ cup orange juice)
¼ cup sesame tahini
1 tablespoon cinnamon

1. Soak prunes in apple juice.

2. Peel, core and chop apples.

3. In a covered pot, bring prunes, apples, apple juice and salt to a boil. Reduce heat and simmer for 30 minutes.

4. Remove zest and squeeze juice from the oranges. Set each aside.

5. Add orange juice, tahini and cinnamon to the cooked apple mixture and blend until smooth. A food processor works best.

6. Stir in orange zest and set aside.

Top and bottom layers

1 cup raw walnuts

2 cups gluten-free or regular rolled oats

2 cups brown rice flour

½ teaspoon sea salt

½ cup dried maple sugar

2 teaspoons cinnamon

½ cup safflower oil *(see Prep Notes for oil-free option)*

1 tablespoon vanilla extract

¾ cup apple juice

1. Preheat oven to 350 degrees.

2. Toast walnuts, oats, and flour in the oven on separate baking sheets; remove each when slightly browned and aromatic.

3. Chop walnuts with food processor (or with a knife), but stop before they become powder. Leave some small chunks.

4. Partially blend oats.

5. Mix all top and bottom layer ingredients together in a bowl.

6. Oil a 9 x 12 inch glass baking dish.

7. Spread out ⅔ of mixture into the baking dish and press down.

8. Spread the apple plum filling out evenly on top of the baked bottom layer and crumble the remaining topping over the filling.

9. Bake at 350 degrees for 50 minutes.

Orange Topping

2 medium oranges

4 cups unsweetened rice milk

¾ cup brown rice syrup

¼ cup pure maple syrup

5 tablespoons agar-agar flakes

Pinch of sea salt

1 teaspoon vanilla extract

1. Remove zest and juice from oranges. (½ cup juice) Set aside.

2. Combine the rice milk, syrups, agar-agar and salt in a pot. Bring to a boil. Whisk to dissolve the agar-agar. Remove from heat.

3. Whisk in orange juice, orange zest and vanilla.

4. Pour into a bowl to cool.

5. After cooled, puree with a blender. Refrigerate. The sauce will thicken as it sits.

6. Drizzle on each piece just before serving.

I am lucky enough to be able to take this amazing food for granted. I cannot remember what it was like not to go to Friday Night Dinners, but even more important than the nourishing food I've grown up on is the loving and supportive community who shared it with me!

— **Rommia White**

(age 19 — coming to dinners since age 2)

April

(left) *Tofu, Carrot and Avocado Nori Rolls in process.*
(above) *Meena in the kitchen.*

Kidney Bean and Yam Soup

PREP NOTES: Garnet or jewel yams are beautiful and delicious in this soup. Red chili beans substitute nicely for the kidney beans.

4 cups uncooked red kidney beans

1 four-inch strip kombu or kelp

3 medium yellow onions, diced (~4 cups)

2-3 tablespoons water

1 tablespoon dried basil

6 medium carrots, diced (~3 cups)

6 large yams (sweet potatoes), peeled and diced (~10 cups)

3 quarts water

1 teaspoon sea salt

Dash of black pepper

3 tablespoons brown rice miso

3 tablespoons sweet white miso

½ pound fresh spinach

1. Soak beans overnight with 8 cups of water and the kombu.

2. Rinse beans and place in a large pressure cooker, or large pot, with kombu or kelp and fresh water to cover beans by 1 to 2 inches.

3. Bring to boil and skim off any foam. Secure lid and pressure-cook for 45 minutes or less depending on your pressure cooker. Boiling in a pot needs at least 60 minutes of cooking time. After beans are cooked, drain and save bean water. Dice sea vegetable.

4. In a large 8 quart pot, sauté onions and basil in water for a few minutes until the onions are translucent.

5. Add carrots, sweet potatoes, and any combination of bean water from the cooked beans, along with fresh water that adds up to 3 quarts.

6. Bring to boil and then turn the heat down to simmer; cover, and cook for 30 minutes.

7. Add beans, diced sea vegetable, salt, pepper and misos, and simmer for another 30 minutes.

8. Remove stems from spinach, chop well, and garnish each bowl of soup with the spinach and serve.

Nori Rolls

PREP NOTES: Two combinations of nori rolls are offered in this recipe. Many other combinations of ingredients can be used inside nori rolls. They can be as simple as carrots and cucumbers, or they can even contain leftovers to make a great take-along lunch. To make this oil-free, broil the tempeh and tofu. First, slice and toss with the tamari. Then place on a baking sheet and broil until browned on all sides. *See page 76 for photo of Tofu, Carrot and Avocado Roll.*

4 cups short grain brown rice

5 cups water in a pressure cooker, or 6 cups if boiling

½ teaspoon sea salt

20 sheets of nori

Bamboo sushi mat (optional)

Tempeh, Sauerkraut and Kale

½ pound soy tempeh

2 teaspoons toasted or regular sesame oil

2 teaspoons wheat-free or regular tamari

16 ounces sauerkraut

2 tablespoons sesame tahini

2 large bunches kale

Tofu, Carrot and Avocado

¾ pound firm tofu

½ tablespoon toasted or regular sesame oil

2 teaspoons wheat-free or regular tamari

4 medium carrots

2 ripe avocados

1 tablespoon umeboshi plum paste

Preparing the filling

1. Cook the rice in the appropriate amount of water with salt. Set aside for about 1 hour. It rolls best when warm.

2. Prepare tempeh, slicing into strips ¼ inch thick by ¼ inch wide by 7 inches long.

3. Sauté tempeh in toasted sesame oil until brown on all sides. Sprinkle with 2 teaspoons of tamari and turn a few more times. Set aside.

4. Prepare the tofu in the same manner as the tempeh. Set aside.

5. Slice carrots into long strips, ¼ inch by ¼ inch by 7 inches long. (Shorter is fine; combine several pieces when laying out to roll.)

6. Bring 2 quarts of water to a boil. Blanch carrots until tender and remove from the boiling water and set aside to cool.

7. Rip the kale leaves from the tougher stems. Blanch kale leaves until tender, but still bright green. Cool in a bowl of cold water, strain, and squeeze out excess water. Chop coarsely and set aside.

8. Put the sauerkraut in a colander to remove excess liquid; place strained sauerkraut in a bowl and mix tahini in. Set aside.

9. Cut each avocado in half, lengthwise. Remove the pit. Carefully slice the flesh into ¼ inch thick crescents without cutting the skin. Scoop the slivered flesh from the outer skin with a spoon.

Rolling Nori

1. Place nori on the bamboo mat, or rolling surface, with shiny side down.

2. Nori is best rolled when rice is warm. Scoop out about ½ cup of rice and gently press and spread onto a sheet of nori, leaving the top inch uncovered.

3. For each Tofu, Carrot and Avocado roll, use a butter knife to spread a strip of about ¼ teaspoon of umeboshi paste on the horizontal center of the rice. The umeboshi is not needed for the Tempeh, Sauerkraut and Kale roll, as the sauerkraut carries a sour and salty taste.

4. With the uncovered part of the nori the furthest away, pick up the closest edge of the mat and nori together and begin to roll.

5. It helps to tuck the end you are working with firmly into the center, while bending the mat slightly up.

6. Continue to roll applying pressure down and toward yourself, until reaching the uncovered part of the nori. Here, give a little more compression to the roll by holding the end closest with one hand, and the furthest end with the other hand, and pull the roll even tighter. Now, roll the rest of the way, and continue to wrap the sushi mat over the roll.

7. Finish rolling and hold the nori roll tightly in the mat a moment to seal the edges. Set on a platter, or tray, with the seam down.

8. Cut each roll into 8 to 10 pieces with a sharp knife. Serve 3 or 4 slices of each variety.

Ginger Tamari Dipping Sauce

PREP NOTES: Place in small bowls with spoons for each table to share. This sauce is great in a stir-fry.

½ cup wheat-free or regular tamari

¾ cup water

1 teaspoon fresh ginger root, finely grated or minced

1 large clove garlic, minced

1½ tablespoons pure maple syrup

1 teaspoon mirin (rice cooking wine)

1. Mix all ingredients together.

2. Allow a half hour or more for the flavor to develop.

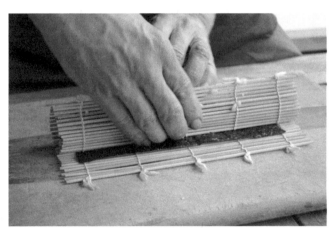

Purple Cabbage Salad

PREP NOTES: The color of this press is quite beautiful and makes a strong statement on the plate.

    2 medium heads red cabbage
    2 teaspoons sea salt
    ½ cup brown rice syrup
    2 tablespoons brown rice vinegar

1. Slice red cabbage into thin strips.

2. Using hands, mix salt thoroughly into red cabbage.

3. Press in a large bowl. A ceramic bowl with steep edges works best. Place a plate on top that is just slightly smaller than the diameter of the bowl. Place a weight on top. A glass gallon jug full of water works great, or another bowl or pot filled with water. *See photo on page 69.*

4. Press the cabbage for at least 4 hours. No refrigeration necessary.

5. When done, rinse any salt off.

6. Mix in brown rice syrup and vinegar.

Blanched Broccoli with Lemon

6 heads broccoli with stems
1 lemon

1. Prepare broccoli by cutting or peeling away the hard outside stalks, leaving the soft inside stalks attached to the heads.

2. Slice both the stalk and head into long sections.

3. Blanch until dark green and soft, but not mushy.

4. Juice the lemon and toss with broccoli.

Carrots, Parsnips, Burdock and Sunflower Seeds

PREP NOTES: The exact quantity of vegetables, in cups, is not as important as the proportion. The burdock may have a dark skin. Simply, wash it well. There is no need to peel it.

> 10 medium carrots
> 4 medium parsnips
> 3 (10-inch long) burdock roots
> 2 teaspoons toasted sesame oil (or water)
> 3 to 4 tablespoons water
> Pinch of sea salt
> 1 cup raw sunflower seeds

1. Cut carrots, parsnips and burdock into ¼ inch by ¼ inch by 2 inch long slivers, also called large matchsticks.

2. Toast sunflower seeds in pan on the stove over low flame. Turn often and remove when the seeds are slightly browned.

3. In a large frying pan, sauté burdock with toasted sesame oil, or water on low heat for 5 minutes with a cover on. Stir a couple of times.

4. Add the carrots and parsnips with 3 or 4 tablespoons of water and a pinch of sea salt. Cook until soft, about 10 to 12 minutes.

5. Remove from heat and gently stir in sunflower seeds.

It's a celebration of life, friendship, family and food, with a fantastic dessert to top it all off.

—**Tim Drake**
Director of Primitive Pursuits, an outdoor education program

Steamed Kabocha Squash with Walnuts

PREP NOTES: Kabocha squash is sweet, rich and very sustaining. It is like dessert. We add a pinch of salt to bring out the sweet flavor.

    3 medium kabocha squash
    1 cup raw walnuts
    ¼ cup water
    Pinch of sea salt

1. Leaving skins on, chop squash in half, from top to bottom, and scoop out the seeds.

2. Cut into half moon slices, ½ to 1 inch thick; generally, following the growing lines of the squash.

3. Arrange in a large heavy-bottom frying pan (preferably cast iron) with a quarter cup of water; sprinkle with salt and cover with tight fitting lid.

4. Steam on a medium flame for about 15 minutes, or until soft. Ideally, the squash will finish cooking just as the water is evaporated. If the water disappears and the squash is not cooked, add a little more water to the pan.

5. Toast the walnuts in a pan, or in the oven, and coarsely chop.

6. Garnish with walnuts and serve.

Spiced Pear Peanut Flan

PREP NOTES: Pears and peanuts are an awesome combination! The bottom mixture needs at least an hour to gel before the second layer can be added. This recipe requires 20 small bowls, cups or glasses. Agar powder can be substituted for the flakes at ¼ the volume. If using powder, whisk thoroughly to avoid clumping.

8 ripe pears (Bartlett best)
2 quarts pure pear juice
1 cup brown rice syrup
Pinch of ground cloves
1 teaspoon powered ginger
1 teaspoon nutmeg
1 teaspoon cinnamon
Pinch of sea salt
10 tablespoons agar-agar flakes
1 teaspoon vanilla extract
¾ cup smooth unsalted natural peanut butter
1¾ cups pure maple syrup
1 cup raw unsalted peanuts

1. Peel, core and slice pears into thin crescents.

2. In a large pot, heat pears, pear juice, rice syrup, spices and salt for 20 minutes on a medium flame until soft, but not mushy.

3. Add agar-agar, whisk to help dissolve, bring to a boil and let boil for 2 minutes.

4. Remove from heat and add vanilla.

5. Place half of this mixture into 20 parfait glasses, distributing half of the pears evenly in the glasses. Place the other half of the mixture and pears in a separate bowl, saved for a second layer. Let everything gel, which will take at least an hour. Refrigerating will hasten the process.

6. When the bowl of pear mixture is gelled, mix it with the peanut butter and maple syrup in a blender until creamy.

7. Pour this peanut butter mixture onto the now gelled layer in the parfait glasses.

8. Toast the peanuts in a pan using a low flame, or in the oven until brown and fragrant, for about 5 minutes. Chop the peanuts coarsely and distribute on top.

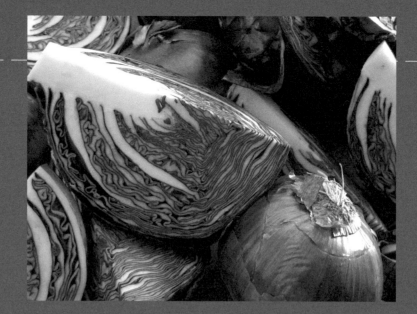

May

{ 91 }

(left) *Ingredients for Collards and Leeks with Roasted Pumpkin Seeds.*
(above) *Vegetables used in Red Cabbage Sauté.*
See a full plate from this menu on page 208.

Gingered Broccoli Noodle Soup

PREP NOTES: This soup pleases everyone. Sautéing the tofu is optional, but doing so adds flavor and richness. For an oil-free soup, simply omit this step. An 8-quart pot is needed.

3 medium heads broccoli (7 to 8 cups)

1 (12-ounce) package of small rice noodles

4 quarts water

2 two-inch pieces of wakame or alaria seaweed

16 ounces firm tofu, cut in ¼ to ½ inch cubes

1 tablespoon toasted sesame oil (optional)

¾ cup wheat-free or regular tamari

2 medium onions, diced small (~2½ cups)

4 tablespoons fresh ginger root, minced or finely grated

3 tablespoons mirin (rice cooking wine)

6 medium carrots, diced (~3 cups)

4 medium parsnips, diced (~2 cups)

1. Separate broccoli stems from tops. Remove tough outer layer from stems and cut stems into bite-sized pieces. Set aside.

2. Separate broccoli tops into bite-sized pieces and set aside.

3. Cook, strain and cool noodles. Set aside.

4. Sauté tofu in sesame oil for 3 to 4 minutes. Add 4 teaspoons tamari and sauté another 3 to 4 minutes. Set aside.

5. Place wakame or alaria seaweed in 4 quarts of water and bring to a boil.

6. Lower heat to medium, add onions and cook for 10 minutes.

7. Remove sea vegetable and cut into small pieces, returning it to the pot.

8. Add ginger, remaining tamari and mirin.

9. Continue cooking on medium heat for 5 minutes.

10. Add carrots, parsnips and stems of broccoli. Cook for 2 minutes.

11. Gently stir in noodles. Cook for 1 minute.

12. Add broccoli tops. Simmer until broccoli is tender, about 2 or 3 minutes.

Black Beans with Roasted Onions

PREP NOTES: We are fortunate to be able to use the most wonderful local black beans from Cayuga Pure Organics, grown just a few miles down the road. Ithaca renowned Macro Mama herself, Peggy Aker, reminded us how sweet onions become with low-heat oven roasting. A large hotel pan is needed, with dimensions of 20 by 12 by 2½ inches, or the equivalent in glass casserole dishes.

> 4 cups dried black beans
> 1 four-inch strip of kombu or kelp
> 4 medium onions, diced small (~5½ cups)
> 2 or more tablespoons water
> 5 cloves garlic, minced
> 1 tablespoon dried basil
> 1½ tablespoons cumin
> 1 teaspoon sea salt

1. Soak beans overnight with kombu or kelp and 2 quarts of water.

2. Rinse beans and place in pressure cooker with the same piece of sea vegetable and enough water to cover the beans by 1 to 2 inches.

3. Bring the beans to a boil and skim off the foam. When the foaming stops, place lid on the pressure cooker. Bring to pressure, turn the flame down low and cook until done. The beans cook 50 minutes or less depending on your pressure cooker. If cooking the beans in a regular pot with a lid, it will take an additional 30 minutes.

4. In a large hotel pan, combine onions, 2 tablespoons of water, garlic, basil, cumin and salt. Bake at 325 degrees for 1 hour, stirring occasionally, and possibly adding a few more tablespoons of water to prevent the onions from drying out.

5. After beans are cooked, and the pressure has come down, drain, save the liquid, remove sea vegetable and chop well.

6. Mix onion mixture and sea vegetable into hot beans, adding enough bean liquid to make the beans moist, but not wet. Serve.

*When everyone helps just a
little, we achieve so much!*

—Daniel Keough
Public Health Advocate

Broiled Polenta

PREP NOTES: This is one of our guests' all-time favorite dishes. It is easy to make oil-free. Simply eliminate the oil from the glaze, still broiling with the rice syrup and salt. Two baking sheets are needed.

> 10 cups water
> 1⅓ cups brown rice syrup
> 1⅓ tablespoons sweet white miso
> 1⅓ teaspoons sea salt
> 4 cups yellow corn grits
> 2 cups fresh corn (10 ounces frozen corn)

> ### Glaze for broiling
>
> 2 teaspoons olive oil (optional)
> 2 teaspoons brown rice syrup
> 2 pinches of sea salt

1. In a large pot, add water, rice syrup, miso, and salt.

2. Bring to a boil and simmer on low heat for 10 minutes.

3. Whisk or stir in corn grits.

4. Cook for 10 minutes, stirring almost constantly with a wooden spatula. Watch that the bottom does not burn.

5. Stir in corn and continue to simmer, remembering to stir constantly as the polenta gets thicker.

6. After 5 minutes, turn heat off and let mixture sit for 30 minutes.

7. Spread the mixture onto 2 baking sheets, with dimensions of about 11 by 15 inches.

8. Bring a small bowl of cold water to your work area. Using the water to moisten your hands, spread the mixture in the pan to create an even surface in the pan.

9. Stir glaze ingredients together and distribute evenly onto the surface of the mixture in both pans by rubbing by hand, or with a rubber spatula.

10. Broil until a nice golden crust appears. Watch carefully so it does not burn. It takes only a few minutes to broil, depending on the pan's distance to the broiler. If you do not have a broiler, use the oven at the highest setting.

11. Keep warm in oven until serving, but not too long, as it will dry out.

12. Cut each sheet into 16 squares.

Steamed Asparagus, Cauliflower and Carrots with Orange Sesame Dressing

PREP NOTES: With this combination of vegetables, getting the sizes to match is integral to the final creation.

1½ pounds asparagus
8 medium carrots, peeled
1 large cauliflower

1. Cut asparagus into 3 inch sections, discarding the tough ends.

2. Cut carrots to match the shape of asparagus.

3. Cut cauliflower into bite-sized pieces, following the growing pattern of the vegetable.

4. Steam vegetables separately.

5. Toss steamed vegetables with Orange Sesame Dressing.

Orange Sesame Dressing

Juice of 3 oranges (~¾ cup)
4 tablespoons sesame tahini
Pinch of sea salt
¼ cup fresh finely chopped parsley
Water if needed

1. Mix or whisk orange juice, tahini and salt together until smooth. Add chopped parsley and stir.

2. If dressing is too thick, wisk in a few tablespoons of water.

Pressed Spring Salad with Pecans

2 small young green cabbages, diced

6 green scallions, diced small

1 bunch fresh chives, diced small (~¼ cup)

½ pound spinach, chopped small

1 bunch assorted radishes, diced small

1 teaspoon sea salt

¼ cup raw pecans

1. Mix salt thoroughly into vegetables by hand.

2. Press in a large bowl. A ceramic bowl with steep edges works best. Place a plate on top that is just slightly smaller than the diameter of the bowl. Place a weight on top. A glass gallon jug full of water works great, or use another bowl or pot filled with water. Press for 4 or more hours. *See photo on page 69.*

3. Toast pecans in pan on stovetop, or on a sheet in oven, and chop small.

4. Rinse salt off and toss toasted pecans in.

The food is delicious, and the company is nourishing. Going to Friday Dinner is like coming home, but without the dishes.

—Sherry Colb
Cornell University Law Professor

Collards and Leeks with Toasted Pumpkin Seeds

Prep Notes: Greens, pumpkin seeds and umeboshi plum are an excellent combination that bursts with flavor.

    1 cup raw pumpkin seeds
    6 medium leeks
    3 bunches collards, cut into large bite-sized pieces
    2 tablespoons umeboshi plum vinegar

1. Toast pumpkin seeds in pan on stovetop, or on baking sheet in oven.

2. Prepare leeks by cutting entirely in half lengthwise and cleaning well under running water. Slice horizontally into large bite-sized sections.

3. Blanch leeks for 5 to 7 minutes.

4. Blanch collards for 2 to 4 minutes.

5. Toss with vinegar and pumpkin seeds.

Red Cabbage Sauté

PREP NOTES: This cabbage dish is actually quite sweet. It needs to be watched carefully, as the onions on the bottom are easy to burn.

- 6 medium red onions, cut into long half-moon slivers
- 2 medium red cabbages, cut into long thin strips
- 6 tablespoons brown rice vinegar
- 2 teaspoons sea salt
- ~¼ cup water

1. In a large pan, sauté onions with a couple of tablespoons of water until translucent.

2. Add the red cabbage and sprinkle with sea salt and vinegar. Add a few tablespoons water and cover.

3. Cook 20 to 30 minutes on low heat, adding small amounts of water as needed. Do not stir.

4. Gently stir together and serve.

Lemon Tart with Blackberry Topping

PREP NOTES: This recipe makes 3 (9-inch) pies, which serves 20 to 27 people. To make this oil-free, simply omit the crust, gel the bottom in parfait glasses, and layer on the cooled topping. Agar powder can be substituted for the flakes, at ¼ the volume. If using powder, whisk longer and thoroughly to avoid clumping. When putting together a shopping list, look at both parts of this recipe as the following ingredients are used more than once: almonds, maple syrup, rice syrup, almond extract, vanilla extract, lemons, and agar-agar.

Crust

1½ cups raw almonds

2¼ cups gluten-free or regular rolled oats

2¼ cups brown rice flour

½ teaspoon sea salt

¾ cup safflower oil

½ cup pure maple syrup

½ cup brown rice syrup

½ teaspoon almond extract

¾ cup water

1. Place almonds on a baking sheet and toast in oven at 350 degrees for 8 to 10 minutes, until lightly browned all through. Do the same with the oats, toasting them for about 5 to 7 minutes.

2. Blend toasted oats into flour with food processor or blender.

3. Blend almonds until the texture is as fine as flour.

4. In a large bowl, stir almonds, oat flour, rice flour and salt together.

5. In a separate bowl, add remaining ingredients, and then stir into the dry ingredients, mixing it all with a large spoon.

6. Press mixture into 3 oiled pie pans.

7. Bake crusts at 350 degrees until browned, about 25 to 30 minutes.

Lemon Filling

1½ cups raw almonds

4 lemons

6 cups unsweetened almond milk

1½ cups brown rice syrup

1½ cups pure maple syrup

1 teaspoon sea salt

9 tablespoons agar-agar flakes

1½ teaspoons almond extract

1½ teaspoons vanilla extract

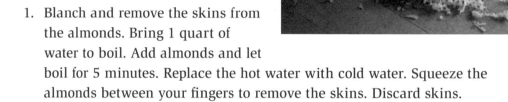

1. Blanch and remove the skins from the almonds. Bring 1 quart of water to boil. Add almonds and let boil for 5 minutes. Replace the hot water with cold water. Squeeze the almonds between your fingers to remove the skins. Discard skins.

2. Remove zest from lemons with a zester or fine grater. Set aside.

3. Squeeze juice from lemons ($\sim$¾ cup).

4. In blender, mix together almonds, almond milk, syrups, salt and lemon juice.

5. Heat blended mixture in a pot. Add agar-agar and bring to a boil.

6. Remove from heat. Add extracts and lemon zest.

7. Pour into prepared crusts.

8. Set aside until firm.

Blackberry Topping

2 lemons

5 cups blackberries (fresh or frozen)

2¼ cups apple juice

Pinch of sea salt

1½ cups brown rice syrup

6 tablespoons pure maple syrup

6 tablespoons agar-agar flakes

1½ teaspoons vanilla extract

6 tablespoons arrowroot stirred into and dissolved in ½ cup water

1. Remove the zest from the lemons and squeeze juice from lemons (~⅓ cup).

2. Place all ingredients in a pot except arrowroot mixture and lemon zest. Start cooking at medium heat.

3. When the mixture begins to boil, add the dissolved arrowroot, stirring constantly for a minute.

4. Reduce heat, add lemon zest, and stir for a few more minutes. Remove from heat when the fruit mixture starts to thicken.

5. Let cool until thickened, 1 hour or longer. Top the firm pies with this blackberry topping.

6. Refrigerate until ready to serve.

{ 106 }

June

{ 107 }

(left) *Strawberries for garnishing Strawberry Cream Pie.*
(above) *Spinach in Theresa's garden.*

Lentil Soup

PREP NOTES: To make this light soup richer and sweeter, add 2 sweet potatoes, diced small. A large 8 quart pot is needed.

    3 cups green lentils
    4 quarts water
    1 three-inch piece wakame or alaria seaweed
    6 small leeks (~3 cups)
    2 medium yellow onions, diced small (~3 cups)
    2 medium rutabagas (unpeeled is fine), diced small (~4 cups)
    6 medium carrots, diced small (~3 cups)
    6 celery stalks, diced small
    5 tablespoons wheat-free or regular tamari
    ½ teaspoon sea salt
    1 tablespoon sweet white miso

1. Bring lentils, water and seaweed to a boil; reduce to medium heat and cook 10 minutes. Then lower to a simmer and cover. Cook until almost soft for another 30 minutes.

2. Prepare leeks by cutting them entirely in half lengthwise and cleaning well under running water. *See photo on page 100.* Separate the top dark green parts from the white bottoms, keeping both parts. Dice small.

3. Add onions, rutabagas, carrots and white bottoms of leeks and cook for 10 minutes.

4. Add celery and cook 5 minutes.

5. Add green leek tops, salt and tamari and simmer for about 5 minutes more.

6. Mix miso with 2 tablespoons of broth and add to pot. Simmer 3 or 4 minutes, making sure leek greens are soft.

Golden Mochi Croutons

12 ounce package of plain brown rice mochi

1. Cut into ¼ inch cubes.

2. Spread out onto 2 baking sheets, separating pieces ½ inch apart, as these will expand. Bake at 400 degrees for 8 minutes. They are ready when puffed and golden brown.

3. Add a few croutons to each bowl of soup just before serving.

Spinach Quinoa Patties
with Carrot Sunflower Dressing

PREP NOTES: These patties take some time to prepare and are well worth it. They will take at least 10 minutes per side to pan fry. To avoid the oil, bake at 350 degrees for 20 to 30 minutes, and then turn and bake another 20 minutes.

> 2 cups uncooked quinoa
>
> 4 cups water
>
> 1½ teaspoons sea salt
>
> 3 pounds fresh spinach (~3 cups cooked)
>
> 3 pounds firm tofu
>
> 2 teaspoons ground nutmeg
>
> 1 bunch scallions, minced
>
> Dash of black pepper
>
> Sesame or olive oil (optional)

1. Rinse and strain quinoa. Add water and sea salt.

2. Bring to a boil, turn down to simmer, cover, and cook for 15 to 20 minutes. Allow to cool.

3. Steam spinach. Cool in cold water. Drain and squeeze out any remaining liquid. Chop into small pieces.

4. Crumble up tofu with your hands. Mix all ingredients (except oil) together and squeeze through your fingers to create a workable consistency.

5. Form into patties, about 3 inches in diameter, and ¾ inch thick. They will be a little wet. Have a delicate touch and do a good job of smoothing the surface together.

6. Pan fry in a small amount of oil. Let them cook until brown on the first side before turning, as this will help them to stay together. Do not use a lid. Cook both sides.

7. Serve immediately, or place on a covered baking sheet and hold in the oven at 250 degrees until ready to serve.

Carrot Sunflower Dressing

PREP NOTES: To make this dressing oil-free, steam the onions and carrots together and exclude the sesame oil. This recipe can be made early in the day and kept in the refrigerator.

> 1 large onion, cut in large chunks
> 1 teaspoon toasted sesame oil (optional)
> 6 or 7 medium carrots, peeled and cut in chunks (~3 cups)
> ¾ cup water
> ½ cup raw sunflower seeds
> 1½ tablespoons brown rice vinegar
> ½ cup brown rice syrup
> Pinch of sea salt

1. In a 2 or 3 quart pot, sauté onions with oil or water for 3 to 5 minutes.

2. Add carrots and water. Bring to boil, reduce to a simmer, cover and cook for 10 to 15 minutes, until carrots are soft. Remove from heat.

3. Toast sunflower seeds in a pan on the stovetop on low to medium heat until lightly browned and fragrant. Stir almost constantly to avoid burning. Let them cool.

4. Puree all ingredients together in blender until smooth.

5. Serve warm or cool on top of Spinach Quinoa Patties.

Summer Pasta Salad

PREP NOTES: This recipe can be made early in the day and kept in the refrigerator. There are a large variety of gluten-free pastas available. Of course, if you are not gluten sensitive, any wheat pasta will work just fine. Elbow or spiral noodles are perfect. This salad is great with sautéed tofu. *To sauté tofu, see page 93, step 4 in the Gingered Broccoli Noodle Soup recipe. For an oil-free option for tofu see Prep Notes on page 124.*

3 pounds brown rice pasta
1 pound fresh shelling peas
8 medium carrots
½ head garlic, minced
6 tablespoons sesame tahini
½ cup balsamic vinegar
¼ cup umeboshi plum vinegar
1 bunch scallions

1. In a large pot, bring 6 quarts of water to a boil.

2. Shell and then blanch peas for 2 minutes in boiling water. Remove peas and submerse in cold water; strain.

3. Add pasta to the boiling water and cook until almost done.

4. Cut carrots in small rectangles, or cubes, matching the shape of the pasta.

5. Add carrots and garlic to the cooking pasta and cook 2 or 3 minutes.

6. Drain off cooking water and fill pot again with cold water.

7. When pasta and carrots are cool, drain off water and add peas.

8. In a small bowl, combine tahini, and vinegars. Mix directly into pasta and vegetables.

9. Toss in scallions and serve.

Salad with Radishes, Carrot Flowers and Chive Dressing

2 heads red leaf lettuce
2 heads green leaf lettuce
1 head radicchio
4 medium to large carrots
1 bunch radishes

1. Wash and drain lettuce and radicchio well. Tear lettuce with hands into large bite-sized pieces.

2. Chop radicchio into bite-sized pieces.

3. Make carrot flowers. Peel and then cut thin wedges down the sides of each carrot. Use a knife, or peeler, to sculpt roundness into the carrot between the cut out slices. In this way, form the carrot petals. Then slice horizontally into ¼ inch thick flowers.

4. Depending on the size of the radish, slice into thin rounds or half-rounds.

5. Blanch radishes for 1 minute and plunge into cold water. Drain.

6. Toss all salad ingredients together.

Chive Dressing

1 tablespoon brown rice vinegar
3 tablespoons mirin (rice cooking wine)
4 tablespoons brown rice syrup
½ cup water
1 handful chives (4 tablespoons diced fine)

1. Mix well and toss on salad.

Arame, Red Onion and Pine Nuts

PREP NOTES: The lemon juice brings out the pink color of the onions.

> 3 packed cups dry arame (~2 ounces)
> 2 cups water
> 3 tablespoons wheat-free or regular tamari
> 4 medium red onions
> 1 lemon, juiced
> 4 tablespoons raw pine nuts

1. Soak arame in water for 45 minutes.

2. Simmer arame in soaking water and tamari for 15 to 20 minutes. Leave uncovered to allow evaporation of excess water.

3. Cut onions in half from top to bottom. Continue slicing in the same orientation to create half-moon slivers.

4. Separately boil onions for 1 minute. Remove from the water and add lemon juice to onions.

5. Toast pine nuts on baking sheet in oven, or in pan on stovetop.

6. Remove arame from heat, fold in onions and sprinkle with pine nuts and serve.

Zesty Lemon Cabbage with Caraway

PREP NOTES: The lemon zest adds something special to this late spring salad. Be careful when toasting the caraway seeds, as they burn easily.

- 2 small green cabbages, grated or sliced thinly (~4 cups)
- 1 small red cabbage, grated or sliced thinly (~2 cups)
- 4 scallions, chopped small
- 2 tablespoons raw caraway seeds, toasted lightly in a pan
- 2 teaspoons sea salt
- 2 lemons
- 1 cup parsley, chopped

1. Using hands, mix caraway seeds and salt thoroughly into vegetables.

2. Press in a large bowl. A ceramic bowl with steep edges works best. Place a plate on top that is just slightly smaller than the diameter of the bowl. Place a weight on top. A glass gallon jug full of water works great. Or, use another bowl or pot filled with water. Press for 4 or more hours. *See photo on page 69.*

3. Rinse off salt.

4. Remove the zest from the lemons with a zester or fine grater. Squeeze out the juice and stir both into the press.

5. Fold in parsley.

My belief that really healthy food cannot also taste good waned with the reality of the tasty food in front of me. These dinners are AWESOME. No kidding!

—**Julianna Platek,** Health Advisor

Strawberry Cream Pie

PREP NOTES: Makes three (9-inch pies), with 24 or 27 large slices. Make pies several hours ahead of time, if not the day before. Agar powder can be substituted for the flakes, at ¼ the volume. If using powder, whisk longer and thoroughly to avoid clumping. When putting together a shopping list, notice that almonds and strawberries are used more than once. Making this as a parfait without the crust is a delicious oil-free option.

Crust

1½ cups raw almonds
2¼ cups gluten-free or regular rolled oats
2¼ cup brown rice flour
Pinch of sea salt
¾ cup safflower oil
¾ cup pure maple syrup
¾ cup water

1. Toast almonds and oats separately on baking sheets at 350 degrees until browned.

2. Separately blend almonds and oats into a flour.

3. Mix almond flour, oat flour, rice flour and sea salt together.

4. Whisk wet ingredients together; then mix into the dry ingredients.

5. Have a bowl of cold water nearby to lightly moisten hands when necessary. Press crust mixture into 3 oiled pie pans.

6. Bake at 350 degrees until lightly browned about 15 to 20 minutes.

Naoko Kubomura, our Rotary exchange student from Japan, 2007.

Filling

2 quarts strawberry juice

1 quart apple juice

9 cups fresh strawberries

3 cups brown rice syrup

1½ teaspoons sea salt

1 cup agar-agar flakes

1½ teaspoons vanilla extract

9 tablespoons arrowroot dissolved in ½ cup water

1. In a blender, mix juices, strawberries, rice syrup and salt.

2. In a pot, mix blended ingredients with agar-agar and bring to a boil.

3. Gently whisk in dissolved arrowroot and simmer for 2 to 3 minutes. Turn heat off and whisk in vanilla.

4. Pour ⅔ mixture into baked piecrusts. Cool in refrigerator.

5. Cool remaining mixture in a bowl, to be used for the cream.

Cream

1 cup raw almonds

Cooled juice/strawberry mixture

1. Blanch and remove the skins from the almonds. To do this, bring 2 cups of water to boil, add almonds and boil for 5 minutes. Then remove from heat and replace the hot with cold water. Squeeze the almonds between your fingers to remove the skins. Discard the skins.

2. In a blender, combine blanched almonds with mixture until smooth. Pour onto cooled pies.

Topping

3 cups strawberries

1. Slice berries into pleasant shapes. Decorate pies with berries.

July

{ 121 }

(left) *Cucumber, Dulse and Dill Pickled Salad;* (above) *Cherry Almond Layered Mousse*

Yellow Split Pea and Corn Soup

PREP NOTES: This is a perfect summer soup. The split peas do not need to be soaked and take only 2 hours to cook. Start the peas and then prep everything else. An 8-quart pot is needed.

> 4 cups yellow split peas
> 3 quarts water
> 6 small leeks
> 2 medium yellow onions, diced small (~2½ cups)
> 4 medium carrots, diced small (~2½ cups)
> 8 celery stalks, diced small
> 1 teaspoon sea salt
> 10 ears of corn, cooked and kernels removed (~4½ cups of kernels)
> 4 tablespoons wheat-free or regular tamari

1. Rinse and drain split peas. Place in a large pot, add water, bring to a boil, and then turn down to a simmer. Cook on low heat, covered, for 2 hours. Split peas are easy to burn; check the bottom of the pot occasionally. Using a simple flame-tamer under the pot reduces the chance of burning the bottom.

2. Prepare leeks by cutting them entirely in half lengthwise and cleaning thoroughly under running water. *See photo page 100.* Separate the dark green top parts from the white bottoms, keeping both parts. Dice small. (~4½ cups)

3. When the split peas are soft, add onions, carrots and white bottoms of leeks.

4. Cook for 20 to 30 minutes, until vegetables are soft.

5. Add salt and celery, and cook for 5 more minutes.

6. Add corn, the green parts of leeks, and tamari. Taste the broth. You can always add more tamari to taste, but you can not take it out. Cook for 10 to 12 minutes more.

Tossed Salad with Orange Mint Dressing

1 head green lettuce
1 head red lettuce
1 pound mixed salad greens
½ small red cabbage, grated
4 medium carrots, grated

1. Wash lettuce and drain in colander.

2. Tear gently with hands into bite-sized pieces.

3. Mix all salad ingredients together in a large bowl.

4. Toss with Orange Mint Dressing just before serving.

Orange Mint Dressing

6 oranges
6 tablespoons sweet white miso
2 tablespoons fresh mint, minced
4 scallions, minced

1. Remove 2 tablespoons of zest from oranges.

2. Squeeze the juice from the oranges. (~1½ cup)

3. Whisk orange juice, zest, miso, mint and scallions together until smooth.

Gingered Tofu Triangles with Snap & Snow Peas

PREP NOTES: Fresh peas make this dish absolutely delightful! If toasted sesame oil is not available, use regular sesame oil. If kuzu powder is not available, use 4 tablespoons arrowroot. It is easy to make this oil-free. Instead of sautéing the tofu in oil, use a few tablespoons of the tamari to coat the tofu. Place this tofu on a baking sheet and broil both sides until brown. If a broiler is not available, then baking at a high temperature will also work.

1 quart (¾ pound) fresh snap peas, trimmed

1 quart (¾ pound) fresh snow peas, trimmed

4 pounds firm tofu

2 tablespoons toasted sesame oil *(oil-free instructions in Prep Notes)*

3 tablespoons fresh ginger root, minced or finely grated

1 medium head garlic, minced

1 cup wheat-free or regular tamari

¼ cup pure maple syrup

6 cups water

6 tablespoons kuzu, dissolved in ¼ cup cold water

6-8 scallions, diced small for garnish

1. Blanch snow and snap peas in boiling water for 1 or 2 minutes. Cool immediately in cold water and drain.

2. Cut tofu into triangles, ½ inch thick, 1 to 1½ inches per side.

3. Heat some of the toasted sesame oil in a large frying pan on medium heat. Sauté as many tofu triangles as will fit on the surface of pan. Cook until brown on both sides and remove from pan. Add a little more sesame oil and continue sautéing until all the tofu is cooked. Set tofu aside.

4. In the same pan, add a few tablespoons of water, and then add ginger and garlic. Water sauté a few minutes, adding small amounts of water as necessary.

5. Add tamari, maple syrup and water.

6. Bring liquid mixture to boil, and then reduce to simmer.

7. Add the tofu and simmer 5 minutes, gently turning it over after 2 or 3 minutes.

8. Slowly pour in kuzu mixture, while stirring gently, to avoid breaking up tofu. Simmer until cloudiness clears, for about 1 or 2 minutes. Remove from heat.

9. Gently stir peas in with tofu mixture.

10. Serve over rice and garnish with scallions.

Roasted Zucchini, Yellow Summer Squash and Carrots

PREP NOTES: Yellow summer squash, zucchini and carrots make for a beautifully colored dish. Steaming assures the middle of the vegetable will be cooked. This can be made without the oil, however the broiling is not the same. Without the oil, the vegetables tend to dry out without browning. To avoid this effect, place the vegetables very close to the broiler and watch carefully.

8 medium green zucchinis
8 medium yellow summer squash
8 medium carrots
1½ tablespoons olive oil or water
Pinch of sea salt

1. Cut vegetables into large slices of round and diagonal shapes, or whatever looks nice. Keep carrots separate. Make the sizes all similar. Steam each type of vegetable separately, until they are just barely soft, but still a bit crunchy.

2. Toss vegetables with oil or water and salt.

3. Spread onto 2 or 3 baking pans and broil for about 10 minutes, gently turning the vegetables a few times. Broil until some of the edges are well done and most of the vegetables are nicely browned.

Cucumber, Dulse and Dill Pickled Salad

PREP NOTES: Allow 2 hours of chilling time for the flavors to merge. *See photo on page 120.*

1 cup firmly packed dulse sea vegetable
3 medium red onions, cut into half moon slivers
12 cucumbers, peeled and sliced into thin rounds
6 tablespoons brown rice vinegar
4 tablespoons umeboshi plum vinegar
4 tablespoons brown rice syrup
10 scallions, diced small
1 small bunch of dill, minced

1. Soak dulse in 1 cup of water for 20 to 30 minutes.

2. Bring approximately 2 quarts of water to boil. Quickly blanch the red onions, just until cooked through. Cool by immersing in cold water, and then drain.

3. Remove the dulse from soaking water and chop. You do not need the rich soaking water from the dulse, but it can feed your houseplants.

4. Mix vinegars and syrup with cucumbers, onions, and dulse.

5. Fold scallions and dill into the cucumber mixture.

6. Keep in a cool place until ready to serve.

Long Grain Brown Rice

5 cups long grain brown rice
10 cups water
½ teaspoon sea salt

1. Rinse rice well.

2. In a 5 or 6 quart pot, bring rice, water and salt to boil.

3. Turn down to simmer and cover.

4. Cook on very low heat, covered for 50 minutes. Then let sit for 10 minutes or more before serving.

Eating together and sharing thoughts and the issues of the day around the table nurtures the heart, while the fresh wholesome food feeds the body.

—**Nancy Meserow,** Attorney *(sitting with Amelia and Isabella)*

Steamed Cauliflower, Kale and Green Beans with Pesto

PREP NOTES: Make the pesto first and keep it tightly covered in the refrigerator. The pesto is also delicious on noodles.

> 2 medium heads cauliflower
> 2 bunches kale
> 1½ pounds green beans

1. Separate cauliflower into large bite-sized flower sections.

2. Remove the bottom of the kale stems. Cut leaves into large bite-sized pieces.

3. Remove tips and tails from the green beans. Cut into lengths to match the kale and cauliflower.

4. Steam cauliflower, kale and green beans separately for 5 to 7 minutes. Pay attention not to over-cook.

Pesto

> 2 cups fresh basil leaves
> ¾ cup parsley without stems
> ¾ cup walnuts lightly toasted
> 2 cloves garlic, minced
> 1 tablespoon brown rice miso
> Pinch of sea salt
> ¾ cup of water

1. Blend or use a food processor to combine all of the pesto ingredients.

2. Place a heaping teaspoon of pesto on each serving of vegetables.

Cherry Almond Layered Mousse

PREP NOTES: The cherry bottom will take a few hours to set. The almond pudding will take 1 hour to set in the refrigerator. This recipe makes 22 to 24 parfait glasses, small bowls, or cups. Agar powder can be substituted for the flakes, at ¼ the volume. If using the powder, whisk longer and thoroughly to avoid clumping. When putting together a shopping list, notice that the following ingredients are used more than once: cherries, cherry juice, brown rice syrup, maple syrup, agar-agar and almond extract.

Cherry Bottom

1½ quarts sweet cherries, pitted and cut in half

1½ quarts of 100% cherry juice (tart works the best)

1 cup brown rice syrup

½ cup pure maple syrup

Juice of 1 large lemon

½ teaspoon sea salt

9 tablespoons agar-agar flakes

1 teaspoon almond extract

3 tablespoons arrowroot powder dissolved in 3 tablespoons of water

1. In a medium-sized pot, combine the cherries, cherry juice, syrups, lemon juice and salt. Bring to a boil.

2. Whisk in agar-agar and boil steadily for 5 minutes.

3. Reduce heat to simmer. Whisk in almond extract and arrowroot mixture. Continue stirring and simmering for 1 to 2 minutes. Remove from heat.

4. Cool for 30 minutes. Then pour ½ cup of mixture into each parfait glass or small bowl. Allow to cool and set before adding pudding.

Almond Pudding

1½ quarts unsweetened almond milk
¾ cup brown rice syrup
8 tablespoons agar-agar flakes
1 teaspoon almond extract
1½ cups raw almonds
¾ cup pure maple syrup

1. Blanch and remove the skins from the almonds. To do this, bring 1 quart of water to boil, add almonds, let boil for 5 minutes, and then place them in cold water. Squeeze the almonds between your fingers to remove the skins. Discard the skins.

2. In a pot, mix together almond milk, rice syrup and salt. Whisk in agar-agar and boil for a few minutes until the flakes dissolve.

3. Stir in almond extract and remove from heat.

4. Let mixture set for 1 hour or longer. Refrigeration speeds up the process.

5. After mixture has set, puree mixture together in a blender with almonds and maple syrup until smooth.

6. Distribute on top of cooled cherry mixture.

Topping

1½ cups toasted slivered almonds
1 pint cherries, pitted

1. Garnish each parfait with a pitted cherry and a circle of toasted slivered almonds.

August

{ 135 }

(left) *Orange Barbecued Tempeh*; (above) *French-Cut Steamed Carrots and Yellow Summer Squash*

Corn Chowder

PREP NOTES: Cornmeal burns very easily. When sautéing the onions and carrots with it, stir frequently. Any type of summer squash can be substituted for the zucchini. If using frozen corn, blend a few cups of the soup at the end of cooking time and stir the blended soup back in.

18 ears of corn (~8 cups)
4 quarts water
2 medium red onions, diced small (~2½ cups)
2 medium yellow onions, diced small (~2½ cups)
1 tablespoon olive oil or water
8 medium carrots, diced small (~4 cups)
3 tablespoons cornmeal
6 celery stalks, diced small
2 small green zucchini squash, diced small (~2 cups)
4 tablespoons sweet white miso
1 teaspoon sea salt
½ bunch fresh parsley, chopped

1. Remove husks and boil corn in 4 quarts of water for 10 minutes. Remove the corn from the pot and keep the corn water. Cool and cut the kernels from cobs. Return cobs to water and simmer for 20 minutes. Remove and discard cobs; keep the cooking water to be used later as the broth.

2. In large 8 quart soup pot, sauté onions in olive oil or water for 2 to 3 minutes.

3. Add carrots and corn meal; sauté for 2 minutes, stirring constantly.

4. Add water from cooked corn and additional fresh water to equal 4 quarts. Simmer for 20 minutes.

5. Add corn kernels, celery, zucchini and cook for 8 to 10 minutes. The celery should be a bit crunchy.

6. Add miso and salt, simmer for 5 minutes.

7. Garnish with parsley when serving.

Orange Barbecued Tempeh

PREP NOTES: Marinating the ingredients with the steamed tempeh will make the flavor richer, for 15 minutes minimum, although an hour is best. *See photo on page 134.*

3 pounds soy tempeh, cut in ¾ inch cubes
6 oranges, juiced (~1½ cups juice)
3 tablespoons brown rice vinegar
3 tablespoons mirin (rice cooking wine)
3 tablespoons umeboshi plum vinegar
6 tablespoons wheat-free or regular tamari
¾ cup brown rice syrup
4 tablespoons pure maple syrup
9 cloves garlic, minced
2 tablespoons fresh ginger root, minced or finely grated
6 tablespoons fresh basil, minced
16 scallions, finely chopped
Dash of pepper

1. Steam tempeh cubes for 15 minutes.

2. Mix all other ingredients together.

3. Add tempeh and toss gently but thoroughly. Marinate for at least 15 minutes.

4. Broil on baking sheets, turning occasionally, until all sides are golden brown and crisp.

Quinoa Tabouli

PREP NOTES: The amount of oil can be adjusted, depending on your preference, or omitted entirely.

5 cups quinoa

10 cups water

2 bunches red radishes

½ cup olive oil (optional)

1 large bunch mint leaves, finely chopped (~½ cup)

6 lemons, juiced (~1 cup)

1 teaspoon sea salt

3 tablespoons umeboshi plum vinegar

6 tablespoons raw pine nuts

6 medium cucumbers, peeled and diced small

1½ bunches fresh parsley, finely chopped (~3 cups loosely packed)

1. Rinse quinoa and strain. Add water. Bring to a boil, reduce heat to low, cover and cook for 20 to 25 minutes. Allow to cool.

2. Prepare radishes. Finely dice, quickly blanch and cool.

3. Mix olive oil, mint, lemon juice, salt and vinegar. Add this mixture to the quinoa.

4. Toast pine nuts in a small skillet on a low flame for a few minutes, stirring frequently.

5. Fold in blanched radishes, cucumbers, pine nuts and parsley.

Baby Bok Choy with Herbed Balsamic Dressing

6-8 large bunches of baby bok choy (~3 pounds)

1. Cut greens into long slender pieces. Stack approximately 3 bok choy leaves and cut them lengthwise from top to bottom. Each piece should have both a white bottom and green top.

2. Blanch for 2 minutes until bright green, chewable and still crunchy.

Herbed Balsamic Dressing

3 tablespoons balsamic vinegar

1 tablespoon fresh thyme, finely minced

1 tablespoon fresh oregano, finely minced

6 tablespoons brown rice syrup

1 tablespoon mirin (rice cooking wine)

2 tablespoons wheat-free or regular tamari

1. Mix together all ingredients.

2. Drizzle onto the blanched baby bok choy.

French-Cut Steamed Carrots and Yellow Summer Squash

8 medium carrots (~4 cups)
8 medium yellow summer squash (~4 cups)

1. Peel carrots and cut, using french roll method, as follows: cut diagonally, roll remaining carrot a little, and cut again to make interesting, slightly irregular big bite-sized chunks.

2. Steam carrots until bright orange, but not mushy, about 5 to 7 minutes.

3. Cut the squash, using the same french roll method. Steam until tender, about 4 to 5 minutes.

4. Mix together and serve. *See photo on page 135.*

Every ingredient that my parents use has a purpose. Growing up, they taught my tongue to appreciate each flavor and how it brought balance to my body. I am the oldest son, so I can clearly remember the early attempts at recipes that never made it in any cookbook. Every year as I got older, the food got better. These recipes are the culmination of years of creativity and patience. Enjoy!

— Jonah Freedman, Elementary Teacher

Green Salad with Red Beet Dressing

PREP NOTES: Any combination of lettuce greens will be fine. This dressing is also delicious served warm on steamed vegetables. The color will liven up any plate of food. To make the dressing even richer, sauté the onion and tofu in a teaspoon of sesame oil for a few minutes before adding the water.

- 1 pound mixed salad greens
- 1 head red leaf lettuce
- 1 head green leaf lettuce
- 1 pound baby spinach

1. Wash, dry and rip lettuce into bite-sized pieces. Toss with mixed salad greens.

2. Mix whole baby spinach evenly into lettuce mixture.

Red Beet Dressing

- 3 medium beets
- 2 medium onions
- 8 ounces firm tofu
- ¼ cup sesame tahini
- ¼ cup brown rice vinegar
- ½ cup brown rice syrup
- ¾ teaspoon sea salt
- 1 cup water

1. Place beets with skins in a pot with enough water to cover. Boil for 30 minutes.

2. Submerge beets in cold water and remove the skins. They will slip off with your fingers; a small knife may help with a few spots. Cut them into large pieces.

3. Cut onions and tofu into large chunks.

4. Place onions and tofu in pot with 1 cup water. Bring to a boil, cover and turn down to simmer. Cook for 10 minutes. Remove from heat, cool and drain.

5. In a blender, mix together beets, water, onion/tofu mixture and all remaining ingredients until smooth.

6. Place a spoonful of dressing on each salad serving.

Green Beans, Shitake Mushrooms and Arame with Toasted Almonds

PREP NOTES: If using fresh mushrooms, 4 cups (½ pound) fresh will replace the 2 ounces dried, and there is no need to rehydrate.

> 4 cups dried arame
>
> 2 ounces dried shitake mushrooms
>
> 1 tablespoon olive oil or water
>
> 4 cloves fresh garlic, minced
>
> 2 tablespoons fresh ginger root, minced or finely grated
>
> 4 tablespoons balsamic vinegar
>
> ½ cup wheat-free or regular tamari
>
> 4 pounds green beans with ends removed
>
> 1½ cups raw almonds, toasted and coarsely chopped

1. Soak arame in 2 cups water for 30 minutes.

2. Soak shitake mushrooms in 1 cup of water for 30 minutes.

3. Simmer arame in soaking water for 30 minutes. Set aside.

4. Cook shitake mushrooms with soaking water on medium heat for 30 minutes. If using fresh mushrooms, skip this initial cooking. Cut into thin slices.

5. Sauté shitake mushrooms with olive oil, garlic, and ginger. Remove from heat.

6. Toss arame with vinegar, tamari and shitake mushroom mixture in a large bowl.

7. Blanch the green beans for 2 or 3 minutes, and then plunge into cold water to preserve crispness. Drain.

8. Mix together arame/shitake mixture, green beans, and toasted almonds.

Theresa's Blueberry Crunch Cake

PREP NOTES: This dessert is similar to a traditional coffee cake. It is impressive that this cake is oil and gluten-free. Bake in three 9-inch round cake pans, which will make 24 to 27 slices. Garnish with fresh blueberries for a nice touch. Brown rice syrup and vanilla are used more then once in this recipe. If necessary, substitute another gluten-free flour for the millet flour.

Dry Ingredients

3 cups brown rice flour

1½ cups gluten-free oat flour

1½ cups millet flour

1 tablespoon baking powder

2 teaspoons baking soda

½ teaspoon sea salt

Wet Ingredients

1 lemon

1 cup brown rice syrup

¾ cup pure maple syrup

1½ cup apple sauce

1 tablespoon vanilla

5 cups fresh blueberries

¾ cup unsweetened soymilk

Crunch Topping

1 cup brown rice syrup

6 tablespoons maple sugar

2½ cups raw walnuts

1 tablespoon vanilla

Pinch of sea salt

1. Preheat oven to 350 degrees.

2. Thoroughly mix the dry ingredients.

3. Remove zest from lemon and squeeze out the juice.

4. Mix lemon juice and zest with the blueberries.

5. In another bowl, mix the wet ingredients except the lemony blueberries.

6. Combine the wet and dry mixtures, mix and then fold in blueberries. Spoon into three 9 inch cake pans.

7. Bake 1 hour at 350 degrees until the center is done.

8. While cake is baking, prepare the topping.

9. Toast and coarsely chop walnuts.

10. Heat up the syrup and mix together with the rest of the topping ingredients.

11. When the cake center is done, remove from oven and gently cover with crunch topping. Continue baking for 10 more minutes.

September

{ 149 }

(left) *Theresa in her garden;* (above) *Delicata Squash Rounds before cooking.*

Carrot Ginger Soup

PREP NOTES: The ginger and curry make this soup unforgettable. Serve hot or cold. Use an 8 quart pot.

3 medium onions, diced (~4 cups)

2 tablespoons sesame oil (optional)

2 tablespoons fresh ginger root, minced or grated

2 teaspoons dried ginger

1 teaspoon curry powder

24 medium carrots, peeled and cut into large chunks (~12 cups)

½ cup brown rice syrup

3 quarts water

1 tablespoon sea salt

¼ teaspoon black pepper

1 bunch parsley, for garnish

1. Sauté onions in sesame oil (or water) for 2 minutes.

2. Add fresh ginger root and spices. Sauté for about 4 minutes more.

3. Add carrots, rice syrup, water, sea salt and black pepper. Bring to a boil.

4. Turn down to a simmer and cover. Cook until carrots are soft, about 20 minutes; allow to cool.

5. Puree in a good blender or food processer. Add more salt or rice syrup, to taste.

6. Garnish each bowl with parsley.

Basmati Rice with Corn, Sunflower Seeds and Dulse

PREP NOTES: This rice dish can be served hot or cold. If served hot, use a 12 by 20 by 2½ inch hotel pan or the equivalent. If serving cold, a large bowl is needed.

> 10 ears of corn, husked
> 5 cups brown basmati rice
> 9 cups water
> Pinch of sea salt
> ½ cup sunflower seeds
> 1 cup dulse sea vegetable

1. Boil or steam corn until done; rinse in cold water.

2. Cut the kernels off the cob (~2 cups).

3. Rinse rice; add water and sea salt and bring to a boil in a large pot.

4. Reduce heat, cover and cook at lowest setting for 50 minutes.

5. Toast sunflower seeds in pan or on a tray in the oven.

6. Place cooked rice into a pan or bowl.

7. Fold corn and toasted seeds into the cooked rice.

8. Toast dulse on stovetop for 8 to 10 minutes, watching carefully as it burns easily.

9. Use suribachi, mortar and pestle, or a food processor to break dulse into small pieces.

10. Fold in dulse and serve.

Chickpeas with Basil

Prep Notes: If you are a garlic lover, add more!

1 quart chickpeas (garbanzo beans)
Water to cover beans
1 strip kombu or kelp, 4 inches long
6 cloves garlic, minced
½ cup loosely packed fresh basil leaves, minced
1½ teaspoons sea salt
6 scallions, diced finely

1. Soak chickpeas overnight with 3 quarts of water and kombu or kelp.

2. Rinse chickpeas; add fresh water to cover by 1 to 2 inches and return sea vegetable to pot.

3. Bring chickpeas to a boil, uncovered; skim off any foam that develops, then pressure cook for 1 hour or less depending on your pressure cooker. Add 30 minutes to the cooking time if boiling without pressure.

4. Drain off and save the water from the chickpeas. Fold garlic, salt, scallions, basil and chopped kombu or kelp into hot chickpeas.

5. Add a small amount of chickpea water back into the chickpeas to ensure the dish is moist.

6. Serve hot or cold.

Delicata Squash Rounds

Prep Notes: Cutting the squash into full round circles makes for a unique display. *See photo of squash rounds before steaming on page 149.*

6-8 medium delicata squash

1. Slice delicata into rounds about 1 inch thick. Do not peel them, do remove the seeds.

2. Place in a steamer with a lid.

3. Steam for 10 to 12 minutes, or until tender (but not mushy).

Friday Dinners are a spiritual and inspirational way to begin the weekend.

—**Stephanie Langer-Liblick,** Vegan Chef & Food Connoisseur
   (with her husband Keith)

Broccoli and Cauliflower
with Tangy Sesame Seed Sauce

PREP NOTES: The tangy sauce is quite distinctive and is lovely with other vegetable combinations.

    1 cup raw unhulled brown sesame seeds
    2 tablespoons umeboshi plum paste
    1½ cup water
    1 teaspoon umeboshi plum vinegar
    3 tablespoons brown rice vinegar
    4 broccoli heads with stalks (~10 cups)
    2-3 small cauliflower heads (~10 cups)

1. Prepare sauce by first toasting sesame seeds on the stovetop over a medium flame. Stir constantly until fragrant and seeds can be crushed between your fingers. Remove and cool.

2. In a blender, combine umeboshi paste, water, vinegars and toasted sesame seeds. Set aside.

3. Peel the outside layer off of the broccoli stalks. Cut both vegetables into large bite-sized pieces, including the broccoli stalks.

4. Blanch vegetables separately, until done but still crisp. Submerge briefly in cold water to stop the cooking. Strain well.

5. Toss vegetables together and top each serving with a tablespoon of sauce.

Pressed Arugula and Cabbage with Lime

PREP NOTES: Arugula is quite flavorful. Lime pulls this press together.

> 2 bunches arugula (4 cups loosely packed)
> 2 small green cabbages (8 cups)
> 6 celery stalks
> 1 bunch radishes
> 2 teaspoons sea salt
> 2 limes, juiced

1. Chop arugula coarsely.

2. Cut cabbage, celery and radish into thin strips.

3. Combine vegetables with sea salt, using your fingers to mix deeply. Save the limes for later.

4. Press vegetables in a large bowl. A ceramic bowl with steep edges works best. Place a plate on top, one that is just slightly smaller than the diameter of the bowl. Place a weight on top. A glass gallon jug full of water works great, or use another bowl or pot filled with water. Press for 4 or more hours. *See photo on page 69.*

5. Rinse salt off and add lime juice.

Sweet Savory Salad
with Lemon Poppy Seed Dressing

PREP NOTES: Lemon and poppy seeds are a brilliant combination.

- 2 cups yellow wax beans, cut into 1 inch sections
- ½ cup raw hazelnuts
- 2 pounds mixed salad greens
- 6 cucumbers with strips of skin peeled away, cut into thin rounds
- 4 medium carrots, grated
- ¼ cup golden raisins

1. Quickly blanch and thoroughly cool wax beans.

2. Toast hazelnuts on a baking sheet in 350-degree oven for 10-12 minutes. Chop coarsely.

3. Toss all salad ingredients together.

Lemon Poppy Seed Dressing

16 ounces firm tofu, cut in large chunks

2 small onions, diced (~1½ cups)

1 teaspoon toasted sesame oil *(optional)*

6 tablespoons raw poppy seeds

6 tablespoons sesame tahini

2 tablespoons umeboshi plum paste

2 lemons, juiced (⅓ cup)

4 tablespoons brown rice syrup

1 cup water

1. Sauté onions with toasted sesame oil (or water) for 3 minutes; add tofu and cook for 6 to 8 minutes, stirring regularly. Let cool.

2. Toast poppy seeds in a skillet on the stovetop until popping and fragrant.

3. In a blender, mix all ingredients together except poppy seeds.

4. Fold seeds in after blending.

5. Serve on individual portions of salad.

Peach Custard with Fresh Blackberries

PREP NOTES: Blackberries grow wild in our back woods, which makes this dessert outrageously enjoyable! This recipe makes 22 to 24 parfait glasses, small bowls or cups, at least 6 ounces each. It is possible to substitute agar powder for the flakes, at ¼ the volume. If using the powder, whisk longer and thoroughly to avoid clumping.

12 to 15 peaches (~5 cups cooked peaches)

2½ quarts peach juice

1 cup brown rice syrup

¾ cup pure maple syrup

2 tablespoons dried ginger

1 tablespoon cinnamon

1 cup agar-agar flakes

1½ teaspoon sea salt

6 tablespoons arrowroot dissolved in 6 tablespoons water

½ cup almond butter

2 teaspoons vanilla

1 quart blackberries

1. Boil peaches in water for 10 minutes.

2. Place in cold water and remove the skins.

3. Cut peaches in half, remove the pits. Slice into long sections. Set peaches aside.

4. In a pot, whisk together juice, syrups, spices, agar-agar and salt.

5. Bring mixture to a boil, turn down the heat and add arrowroot mixture. Simmer for 3 minutes.

6. Pour mixture into a bowl and let cool, allowing it to gel.

7. Combine cooled, gelled mixture with peaches, almond butter and vanilla. Puree in a blender until smooth.

8. Pour into custard bowls and top with fresh blackberries.

October

{ 163 }

(left) *Millet Croquettes;* (above) *Priscilla ladles out Cream of Squash Soup. The cover photo shows a full plate from this menu.*

Cream of Squash Soup

PREP NOTES: This is the simplest of recipes and the taste is amazing. We call it liquid gold in our house. It takes a while to peel and chop squash. A good vegetable peeler will help. In October, squashes are very sweet and may not need the optional brown rice syrup. A parsley garnish on each serving is a nice touch. An 8-quart pot is needed.

> 2 large butternut squashes (~14 cups)
> 4 medium onions, chopped coursely (~6 cups)
> Water to almost cover squash (~2 quarts)
> 1 tablespoon sea salt
> 4-6 tablespoons brown rice syrup *(optional)*
> ½ bunch of parsley

1. Peel squash, cut in half, remove seeds, and chop into large 2 or 3 inch cubes.

2. Water sauté onions, 4 to 5 minutes, add squash, water, and salt.

3. Bring to boil, reduce to simmer; cover and cook until squash is soft, about 20 to 25 minutes.

4. In a blender, carefully puree hot squash, using just enough liquid to blend, possibly not using all of the liquid. Start at a low speed and slowly increase the speed (to avoid hot soup splattering out of the blender). A slightly thick creamy texture is preferred.

5. Add brown rice syrup if needed.

6. Garnish with parsley.

Sweet and Sour Red Beans

PREP NOTES: If baked for an extra hour, covered, this dish will resemble old-fashioned baked beans. Red chili beans are best for this recipe, but kidneys are also very tasty.

6 cups dried red chili beans
1 four-inch strip of kombu or kelp
Water to pressure cook beans
6 tablespoons brown rice miso
½ cup apple juice
1½ cups brown rice syrup
3 tablespoons prepared mustard
2 tablespoons brown rice vinegar
1 teaspoon sea salt

1. Soak beans overnight with kombu and 2 times as much water as beans.

2. Rinse soaked beans; add water to cover by 1 or 2 inches, return kombu to the pot, and bring to a boil. Skim off any foam, and then cover. Cook until tender, about 45 minutes or less, depending on your pressure cooker, or an hour if boiling.

3. When beans are soft, drain liquid, saving 2 cups of the liquid, plus the kombu or kelp. Place beans in a large pot or in a 9 by 12 inch baking dish. Dice sea vegetable and mix with beans.

4. Combine remaining ingredients with the 2 cups of bean liquid and add to beans.

5. Simmer uncovered for 45 minutes, or bake uncovered at 350 degrees for 1 hour, gently stirring now and then.

Grated Daikon and Carrot Salad

⅓ cup raw unhulled brown sesame seeds

4 medium daikon radishes (6 cups grated)

12 medium carrots (6 cups grated)

2 tablespoons umeboshi plum vinegar

6 tablespoons brown rice vinegar

1. Toast sesame seeds in pan at medium heat for 5 to 10 minutes while stirring frequently. They are done when seeds start to pop and can be crushed between your fingers.

2. Grate daikon radishes and carrots.

3. Mix all together and serve.

Millet Croquettes with Orange Miso Sauce

PREP NOTES: These patties are "the rave" at our dinners. Allow 1 hour for the millet to cool after cooking. These can be served immediately after pan-frying or keep warm in the oven. However, do not hold in oven longer than 1 hour as they will get too dry. Makes about 25 croquettes. To make oil-free, after forming, place patties on a baking sheet and bake for 30 to 40 minutes at 350 degrees. *See photo on page 162.*

3 cups millet, washed and strained

7 cups water

1 teaspoon sea salt

2 medium onions, diced small (~2 cups)

3 medium carrots, grated (~1½ cups)

⅓ cup raw sunflower seeds, toasted

4 tablespoons wheat-free or regular tamari

1 tablespoon umeboshi plum vinegar

1 bunch parsley, chopped

Olive oil or sesame oil for frying *(see Prep Notes for oil-free option)*

1. Rinse millet well, add water, salt and bring to a boil.

2. Reduce heat to low, cover and cook for 25 minutes.

3. Move the hot millet to a large bowl and stir in onions.

4. After cooling somewhat, add all other ingredients except parsley.

5. When cool enough to handle, mix well by squeezing the millet through your fingers.

6. Taste and adjust for salt, tamari, and vinegar. Mix in the parsley.

7. Place a small bowl of cold water nearby. This will make it easier to form patties.

8. Dip your hands briefly in the water and form fistfuls of mixture into patties, about 3 inches in diameter by ¾ to 1 inch thick. They will be easier to fry if the top and bottom surfaces are fairly flat.

9. Pan fry in a thin layer of oil, browning one side, and then flip and brown the other.

10. Serve immediately or hold in a warm oven on a baking pan or dish.

Orange Miso Sauce

PREP NOTES: This sauce is an exquisite addition to these scrumptious croquettes.

4 tablespoons sweet white miso
4 oranges juiced (1 cup juice)
6 tablespoons brown rice syrup
1 tablespoon arrowroot dissolved in ½ cup water

1. Dissolve miso and rice syrup into orange juice, using a fork or a whisk.

2. Bring to a boil; add arrowroot mixture and stir until it starts to thicken. Remove from heat. Allow to cool.

3. Serve about 1 tablespoon of sauce on each croquette.

Teaching about the connection between the foods we eat and our long-term health was one of the greatest gifts my parents gave to me. Understanding that I can take control of my own health destiny via good nutrition has been a comfort and a blessing for which I will be forever grateful.

—**Talia Fuhrman,** Nutrition Journalist

Hiziki with Tempeh, Red Onions, Leeks and Ginger

PREP NOTES: Start by soaking the hiziki in water for 1 hour or longer. A large cast iron pan works well for this dish. Half-moon slices are long vertical cuts with the growing lines of the onion.

1½ cups hiziki sea vegetable, soaked in 3 cups water for one hour
1 pound soy tempeh
4 medium leeks
4 medium red onions, sliced into thin half moons
2 tablespoons fresh ginger root, grated or minced
4 tablespoons wheat-free or regular tamari
1 tablespoon water for sauté

1. Slice tempeh into rectangles, 1½ inches long, by ¾ inch thick, by ½ inch wide. Toss 2 tablespoons of tamari with the tempeh and place on a baking sheet. Broil until browned on both sides.

2. Prepare leeks by cutting them entirely in half lengthwise and cleaning well under running water. *See photo page 100.* Separate the top dark green parts from the white bottoms, keeping both parts. Cut across horizontally in ½ inch wide half moons.

3. Water sauté onions and ginger in 1 tablespoon water for 3 minutes.

4. Add white parts of leeks to onions; sauté 2 minutes longer, saving greens for later.

5. Drain off extra water from the soaked hiziki, saving the water.

6. Add hiziki and ¼ cup of hiziki soaking water to the onions and leeks, and cover. Cook on low heat for 30 minutes.

7. Add tempeh, greens of leeks and 2 tablespoons tamari; simmer for 3 to 5 minutes.

Mixed Greens with Lemon Vinaigrette

PREP NOTES: The vegetables have different cooking times, so boil separately. Also, do not boil too many of each vegetable at one time. This should be the last dish you prepare, so the greens are warm and not overcooked, since the mustard greens can loose their nice green color very quickly. An option is to cool the mustard greens quickly after cooking, and then mixing in with the other vegetables at the last minute.

> 4 bunches collard greens
> 2 bunches mustard greens
> 1 green nappa cabbage
> 6 stalks celery

1. In a large pot, bring 3 quarts of water to a boil.

2. Remove ends of collards and mustard greens, cutting the remaining leaves into large bite-sized pieces.

3. Chop the cabbage into similar sized pieces as the greens.

4. Diagonally cut the celery.

5. Blanch the vegetables in separate batches until tender, but still bright green.

Lemon Vinaigrette

> 3 lemons, juiced (~½ cup juice)
> 2 tablespoons brown rice vinegar
> 2 tablespoons mirin (rice cooking wine)
> ½ cup water
> Pinch of sea salt

1. Mix all ingredients together.

2. Toss with blanched greens.

Steamed Yams & Rutabagas with Maple Walnuts

PREP NOTES: Normally, we do not peel vegetables; however, we do in this recipe to bring out the beautiful orange color of the yams and yellow rutabagas. Garnet and jewel sweet potatoes (often called yams) have a deep orange color and are exceptionally sweet. The goal is to have equal proportions of the vegetables, so adjust depending on the size of the rutabagas.

> 1 cup raw walnuts
> 2 tablespoons pure maple syrup
> 10 medium yams, peeled and cut into large chunks
> 6 medium rutabagas, peeled and cut into large chunks

1. Thoroughly mix syrup with walnuts.

2. Toast walnuts in oven until lightly browned, about 10-12 minutes at 325 degrees. Stir the walnuts occasionally so they do not stick to each other or the pan.

3. Chop walnuts coarsely.

4. Steam yams and rutabagas separately. The rutabagas will take a little longer to cook.

5. Gently mix together vegetables and walnuts.

Apple Crumb with Almond Whip

PREP NOTES: A large hotel pan is needed, measuring 20 by 12 by 2½ inches or its equivalent. When putting together a shopping list, notice that the following ingredients are used more than once in this recipe: apple juice, rice syrup, and maple syrup. For a no oil option, use the crisp topping of December's pear dessert.

Filling

20 to 24 medium apples
1 cup apple juice
1½ cups brown rice syrup
1 tablespoon cinnamon
1 teaspoon nutmeg
1 teaspoon sea salt
4 tablespoons arrowroot dissolved in 6 tablespoons apple juice

1. Preheat oven to 350 degrees.

2. Peel, remove core and cut apples into thin slices.

3. Mix in remaining filling ingredients (except arrowroot mixture) and toss with apple slices. Bake covered for 20 minutes. After removing hot apples from oven, stir in arrowroot that has been dissolved in apple juice.

4. Make crumb topping while apples are baking.

Crumb Topping

PREP NOTES: If using maple syrup instead of maple sugar, add an extra ½ cup of rice flour.

1 cup cornmeal

2 cups brown rice flour

2 cups gluten-free or regular rolled oats

1 teaspoon sea salt

½ cup brown rice syrup

½ cup pure maple syrup

½ cup maple sugar

½ cup safflower oil *(see Prep Notes for oil-free option)*

2 teaspoons vanilla extract

This is what community is all about: great food, great people, and great conversation.

—Jen Majka
Assistant Dean,
Alice Cook House,
Cornell University

The entire meal exploded with flavors and textures I had never before experienced. Delicious is an understatement.

— Eric Lindstrom, Vice President, Marketing, Woodhouse

1. Blend oats into flour with food processor.

2. Stir dry ingredients together in large mixing bowl.

3. Whisk wet ingredients together in separate bowl.

4. Mix wet ingredients into the dry mix.

5. After apples have baked for 20 minutes, and arrowroot mixture has been stirred into apples, evenly distribute crumb topping on top.

6. Bake for 1 hour or longer, at 350 degrees, until the top is evenly golden brown.

Almond Whip

PREP NOTES: Set almond milk gel aside for 1 hour to firm up; then blend all ingredients together. After blending, refrigerate. The complete cooling of the whip adds to the thickness. Agar powder can be substituted for flakes, at ¼ the volume.

> 3 cups unsweetened almond milk
> 4 tablespoons agar-agar flakes
> 1½ cups raw almonds
> 2 teaspoons almond extract
> 1 cup brown rice syrup
> ¼ cup pure maple syrup

1. Boil almond milk with agar-agar for 5 minutes.

2. Pour into a bowl and set aside for an hour or so, until it firms up.

3. Blanch and remove the skins from the almonds. To do this, bring 1 quart of water to boil, add almonds, let boil for 5 minutes; then replace the hot water with cold water. Squeeze the almonds between your fingers to remove the skins. Discard the skins.

4. After gel cools, mix all ingredients together.

5. In a blender, puree until smooth. Refrigerate.

6. For each apple crumb serving, add a spoonful of almond whip on top.

November

(left) *Black Bean Soup;* (above) *Steamed Turnips, Daikon and Carrots with Dulse*

Black Bean Soup

4 cups dried black turtle beans

1 six-inch strip kombu or kelp

3 quarts water (cooked bean liquid can be used)

1 large yellow onion, diced small (~1½ cups)

1 tablespoon dried basil

1 tablespoon cumin

1 teaspoon curry powder

8 cloves fresh garlic, minced

2 tablespoons fresh ginger root, finely grated or minced

4 medium carrots, diced small (~2 cups)

1 large rutabaga, diced small (~2 cups)

8 stalks celery, diced small (~2 cups)

3 tablespoons wheat-free or regular tamari

2 tablespoons mirin (rice cooking wine)

1 tablespoon sea salt

½ bunch fresh parsley

1. Soak beans overnight with kombu or kelp and 2 quarts of water.

2. Rinse beans and place in large pressure cooker with the same piece of sea vegetable and enough fresh water to cover by 1 to 2 inches. Bring to a boil, and skim off any foam. Secure lid and pressure cook for 45 minutes or less, depending on your cooker. If you are not pressure cooking, use a large pot and cook the beans for 75 minutes. Beans should be soft, but not mushy.

3. Sauté onions in a few tablespoons of water in a large pot for several minutes; add spices, garlic and ginger, and sauté 2 or 3 minutes more. Add beans, bean water and enough liquid to equal three quarts added liquid. Cook on medium heat for 10 minutes.

4. Add other vegetables. Cook until they begin to soften, 15 to 20 minutes.

5. Add tamari, mirin and salt and simmer 10 minutes.

6. Garnish with parsley. *See photo on page 178.*

Steamed Turnips, Daikon and Carrots with Dulse

PREP NOTES: If washing does not remove all the dirt, peel vegetables. The dulse sea vegetable pulls this dish together. *See photos on pages 19 and 179.*

6 turnips
8 carrots
1 large daikon radish
½ cup dulse sea vegetable, toasted and chopped coarsely

1. Slice vegetables in half lengthwise and then into 1 inch thick pieces.

2. Steam vegetables separately and then mix together.

3. Sprinkle the vegetables with dulse.

*As we gather together to share a meal,
we are nourished by food, family, and friends.*
—**Cindy Kramer,** Social Studies Teacher

Cranberry Sauce

PREP NOTES: This traditional Thanksgiving staple is tangy and sweet — a real taste sensation. The cranberry sauce will take a few hours to set. It is best to prepare it the day before. If substituting agar powder for the flakes, use ¼ the volume. When using the powder, whisk thoroughly to avoid clumping.

2 lemons
1½ quarts apple juice or apple cider
1½ cups brown rice syrup
⅓ cup pure maple syrup
12 tablespoons agar-agar flakes
6 cups fresh raw cranberries
¾ cup fruit juice sweetened dried cranberries
1 tablespoon cinnamon
½ teaspoon sea salt

1. Remove zest from lemons. Set aside. Squeeze juice from lemons. Set aside.

2. Bring apple juice, syrups and agar-agar to a boil, stirring the agar-agar flakes into the juice until they dissolve.

3. Add the fresh cranberries, dried cranberries, cinnamon, sea salt, and turn the flame down to low.

4. Cover and cook for about 15 minutes until the cranberries are soft.

5. Remove from heat. Stir in lemon juice and zest.

6. Pour into a glass bowl, if you have one, as it looks lovely in this. Let the sauce cool for an hour, then refrigerate to set.

Shitake Tempeh Gravy

PREP NOTES: If using fresh mushrooms, 4 cups (½ pound) fresh will replace the 2 ounces dried, and there is no need to soak in water. It is possible to substitute 4 tablespoons arrowroot for the kuzu. To make without oil, steam tempeh for 10 minutes, crumble it with your hands, and water sauté the onions. This version is thicker and creamier than the oil sautéed version. Both are very good.

2 ounces dried shitake mushrooms

1 pound soy tempeh

4 medium yellow onions, diced small (~5 cups)

2 tablespoons sesame oil *(optional)*

4 cloves garlic, minced

6 cups water

8 tablespoons wheat-free or regular tamari

2 tablespoons mirin (rice cooking wine)

8 tablespoons sesame tahini

6 scallions, diced small

6 tablespoons kuzu dissolved in 6 tablespoons water

1. Soak dried shitake mushrooms in 3 cups of water for 30 minutes.

2. Cut tempeh in half and pan fry in 1 tablespoon sesame oil, browning both sides. *See Prep Notes for oil-free version.*

3. Cook shitake mushrooms with soaking water on medium heat for 30 minutes. Remove the mushrooms and save the water. *Skip this step if using fresh.*

4. Dice the mushroom caps, discarding the stems.

5. Sauté onions, diced shitake mushrooms and minced garlic in 1 tablespoon sesame oil (or water) for 10 minutes.

6. Cut tempeh into ¼ inch thick by ½ inch wide by 1 inch long pieces and add to onion mixture.

7. Add shitake soaking water *or 3 cups of water if using fresh mushrooms*; simmer for 10 minutes.

8. Whisk in tamari, tahini and mirin. Add 3 more cups of water; simmer without a lid for 20 minutes.

9. Add scallions and kuzu. Stir until the cloudiness of kuzu clears and the gravy thickens.

10. Serve over Mashed Millet and Cauliflower.

Mashed Millet and Cauliflower

PREP NOTES: This recipe is a tasty replacement for traditional mashed potatoes. Millet is usually somewhat dirty, so rinse several times until the water is clear.

> 1 large yellow onion, diced small (~1½ cups)
> 3 cups millet, rinsed well
> 1 large head cauliflower (~6 cups)
> 1 teaspoon sea salt
> 9 cups water

1. In a large pot, sauté the onions in 2 tablespoons of water for 3 to 4 minutes.

2. Add rinsed millet and sauté for 5 minutes longer.

3. Chop cauliflower into large pieces. Add to onions with sea salt and water.

4. Bring to boil, uncovered, and then lower heat to simmer. Cover and cook until the millet is tender, about 30 minutes.

5. Mash the mixture together with a hand held potato masher or large wooden spoon.

Wild Rice Stuffed Carnival Squash

PREP NOTES: Wash and drain each type of rice separately before cooking with water. Delicata or acorn squash can be substituted for carnival squash.

12 small to medium carnival squashes

2 cups long grain brown rice

½ cup wild rice

5 cups water

2 pinches of sea salt

2 medium onions, diced small (~2½ cups)

1½ teaspoons sesame oil (optional)

1 teaspoon dried sage or 1 tablespoon fresh sage, minced

2 teaspoons dried basil or 4 tablespoons fresh basil, minced

Pinch of dried or fresh thyme

Pinch of dried or fresh rosemary

½ cup raw pumpkin seeds, toasted

1 cup raw walnuts, toasted and chopped

⅔ cup currants

1 bunch parsley, minced (~1 cup)

3 to 4 stalks of celery, diced small (~2 cups)

2½ tablespoons wheat-free or regular tamari

1½ tablespoons umeboshi plum vinegar

1. Wash and cut the squash in half lengthwise, leaving the seeds in. Place squash on a glass baking dish or stainless baking pan, with the inside facing downward.

2. Sprinkle with a pinch of sea salt. Place ¼ inch of water in the dish. Bake at 350 degrees, until soft, approximately 1½ hours.

3. Wash both types of rice separately. Then combine the rice, and add water and a large pinch of sea salt. Bring to a boil, then cover, reduce heat to low, and cook 45 to 50 minutes.

4. Move rice to a large bowl.

5. Sauté onions in oil (or water) until translucent. Add sage, basil, thyme, rosemary and sauté another 3 minutes. Add this mixture to the cooked rice.

6. Stir in toasted pumpkin seeds, toasted walnuts, currants, parsley and celery.

7. Add tamari and vinegar.

8. When the squash is soft, remove from the oven and scoop the seeds out with a spoon. Place the squash back in the pan, with the inside facing up and fill with a rounded heap of the rice mixture.

9. Bake at 350 degrees for 20 minutes more.

Green Dinosaur and Red Russian Kale with Orange Black Sesame Dressing

PREP NOTES: Dinosaur kale is the common name for lacinato kale. If this kale is not available, any green kale will be fine. However, the dark green of the lacinato kale is striking. It is easy to imagine the strong dose of chlorophyll coming your way.

4 bunches dinosaur kale
3 bunches red russian kale

1. Separate center ribs from the leaves of the kale.

2. Chop ribs separately from leaves in small pieces.

3. Chop leaves into large bite-sized pieces.

4. Blanch rib pieces for 4 minutes.

5. Blanch leaves for 2 or 3 minutes.

6. In a large bowl, toss leaves and rib pieces together.

Orange Black Sesame Dressing

¼ cup unhulled black sesame seeds

4 oranges

4 tablespoons brown rice vinegar

1 tablespoon umeboshi plum vinegar

1 teaspoon brown rice syrup

½ teaspoon fresh ginger root, finely grated or minced

1. Toast sesame seeds in pan until they begin to pop and can be crushed between two fingers. Set aside.

2. Squeeze the juice from the oranges (1 cup juice).

3. Whisk together orange juice, vinegars, rice syrup and ginger root.

4. Add toasted sesame seeds.

5. Fold dressing into blanched greens.

I feel balanced and harmonious when sharing Friday Dinner with others.

—— **Bill White**
Small Business Owner

Pumpkin Pudding with Whipped Soy Cream

PREP NOTES: Traditional fall spices make this dessert a gratifying finale to an autumn feast. Make sure to have a couple of large bowls handy. When assembling a shopping list, notice that the following ingredients are used more than once: tofu, rice syrup, maple syrup, and vanilla. Of the total soymilk in the pudding, 1½ cups is used to blend into the pumpkin mixture; 1 cup is used for dissolving the arrowroot.

> 4 or 5 small pie pumpkins (9 cups puree)
> 1½ teaspoons sea salt
> 12 ounces soft tofu
> 1 cup brown rice syrup
> 1½ cups pure maple syrup
> 1 tablespoon cinnamon
> 1½ teaspoons ginger
> 1½ teaspoons nutmeg
> ½ teaspoon cloves
> 1 tablespoon vanilla extract
> 2½ cups unsweetened vanilla soymilk
> ½ cup arrowroot

1. Preheat oven to 350 degrees.

2. Cut the pumpkins in half lengthwise, leaving the seeds in. Place on a glass baking dish, stainless baking pan, or any baking sheet, with the inside facing downward.

3. Sprinkle with a pinch of sea salt and ¼ cup of water. Bake at 350 degrees, until soft, approximately 1½ hours.

4. Scoop the seeds out and discard. Scoop the flesh out into a big bowl.

5. Mix pumpkin, sea salt, spices, syrups, vanilla and 1½ cups of soymilk in a blender or food processor until smooth.

6. Dissolve ½ cup of arrowroot in the 1 cup of soymilk, making sure to mix thoroughly to remove any clumps of arrowroot. Fold into the pumpkin mixture directly before baking.

7. Bake for 1 hour in a large glass baking dish until the top is golden brown.

Whipped Soy Cream

2 pounds firm tofu
1 cup brown rice syrup
1 cup pure maple syrup
½ teaspoon sea salt
1 tablespoon vanilla extract
1 teaspoon almond extract

1. Boil the tofu for 10 minutes and then rinse under cold water.

2. Squeeze out as much extra water from the tofu as possible by pressing the block in a strainer or inside a cloth napkin.

3. Whip all ingredients together in a blender until smooth.

4. Place a dollop on each serving of pudding.

Priscilla's homegrown pumpkins.

December

(left) *Full plate from this menu*
(above) *Step 4 in the Glazed Sauteed Carrots and Beets recipe*

Creamy Chickpea Soup

PREP NOTES: The creaminess of this broth is developed by blending in some of the chickpeas, which makes this delicious soup unique. A large 8 quart pot is needed.

4 cups chickpeas (garbanzo beans)

1 four-inch piece of kombu or kelp

4 medium leeks

2 large red onions, diced small (~3 cups)

3 medium rutabagas, diced (~3 cups)

6 or 7 medium carrots, diced (~3 cups)

4 medium parsnips, diced (~2 cups)

3 quarts total liquid (cooked chickpea broth and water)

8 tablespoons sweet white miso

1 teaspoon sea salt

1. Soak chickpeas overnight with kombu or kelp, covering the chickpeas with enough water to double the height of the dried beans. Chickpeas absorb a lot of water while soaking.

2. Rinse chickpeas thoroughly and place in large pressure cooker with the same kombu or kelp and enough fresh water to cover chickpeas by 1 to 2 inches.

3. Bring to a boil, without a cover. Skim off foam and, when the foaming stops, lock lid into place; bring to pressure and cook on low heat for 1 hour or less, depending on your cooker. If not pressure cooking, use a large pot and cook chickpeas for 90 minutes.

4. Prepare leeks by first removing the very top of the leaves and the bottom roots. Slice the leeks entirely in half lengthwise, cleaning well under running water. *See photo page 100.* Next, separate the white bottoms from the green tops and dice into small pieces, keeping the white and green sections separate.

5. In a large pot, water sauté whites of leeks and onions for 5 minutes; then add the remaining root vegetables, except the greens of the leeks, cooking for 5 minutes more.

6. In a blender, combine ⅔ of the chickpeas with miso, chickpea broth and enough water to equal 3 quarts of liquid. Set ⅓ of chickpeas aside.

7. Add creamy chickpea mixture to the pot with sautéed vegetables, remaining chickpeas and sea salt.

8. Simmer 20 minutes.

9. Add green ends of leeks and simmer for 5 to 7 minutes and serve!

Friday Dinners are a centerpiece of my health.

—**Dr. Claire Forest,** Director, National Life Coach Program

Kasha Croquettes
with Sweet Scallion Mustard Sauce

PREP NOTES: These patties are truly a labor of love that all will enjoy.
A big cast iron frying pan with a cover works best for cooking the kasha.
Be sure that the pan can hold the kasha and the water together. Separate
kasha into two batches if need be. Makes approximately 24 patties.
These are also very good pan fried in a touch of sesame or olive oil.

4 cups kasha

8 cups water

1½ teaspoons sea salt

2 tablespoons arrowroot

8 scallions, diced small

1. Rinse buckwheat and dry-roast in a frying pan for several minutes.
   Stir frequently.

2. In a separate pot, bring water with salt to a boil.

3. Add boiling water to roasted kasha.

4. Lower to a simmer, cover, and cook for 20 to 25 minutes.

5. Place kasha and arrowroot in a large bowl; stir and allow to cool.

6. When cool enough, add scallions and squeeze mixture through your
   fingers until it holds a shape. This is a delicate process; if kasha
   mixture does not stick together and seems too dry, add a touch more
   warm water.

7. With a bowl of fresh cold water at your side, moisten your hands and
   form kasha into patties, about 3 inches in diameter by 1 inch thick. Be
   sure to have the top and bottom relatively flat, so they will sit without
   breaking apart. Arrange on a baking sheet.

8. Bake at 350 degrees for 40 minutes.

9. Hold in warm oven until served.

Sweet Scallion Mustard Sauce

   1 tablespoon arrowroot

   ¾ cup water

   4 tablespoons prepared mustard

   3 tablespoons sweet white miso

   6 tablespoons brown rice syrup

   4 scallions, minced

1. Dissolve arrowroot in ¼ cup of water.

2. In a small pot, stir or whisk together mustard, miso, brown rice syrup
   and ½ cup water, making sure there are no lumps from the miso.

3. Bring to a slow boil, add arrowroot mixture, and watch sauce thicken
   and clear. Turn off heat.

4. Serve about 1 tablespoon of sauce on each croquette.

Kale with Cranberries and Pecans

1 cup fruit juice sweetened dried cranberries
½ cup apple juice
1 cup raw pecans
6 bunches kale
2 tablespoons umeboshi vinegar

1. Soak cranberries in apple juice for at least 15 minutes, and then strain extra juice and save.

2. Toast pecans on low heat in a pan for about 5 minutes, or on a baking sheet in the oven. Be careful, as pecans burn easily. Chop into large pieces, each about ¼ of pecan.

3. Prepare kale. Remove the hard end stems and discard. Cut out the center ribs.

4. Chop ribs into small pieces.

5. Chop the rest of the kale into large bite-sized pieces.

6. Blanch the ribs and leaves separately. The ribs need to be blanched longer than the leaves.

7. Mix strained apple juice with vinegar.

8. Toss cranberries, nuts and vinegar/juice in with the cooked kale.

Steamed Brussels Sprouts

PREP NOTES: It is especially important to not overcook brussel sprouts, as they easily loose their bright green color.

2 quarts brussels sprouts (~2 pounds)

1. Cut the rough edges and hard stems off the bottom of the sprouts.

2. Steam for about 5 minutes. Brussels sprouts are done when a sharp knife slides in easily. Promptly remove them from the steaming pot. This will allow the excess heat to escape, keeping them from turning a drab green color.

Pressed Dulse Salad
with Lemon Tahini Dressing

PREP NOTES: The lemon tahini dressing is delicious on other vegetable dishes, as a salad dressing, or with any noodle or grain.

    6 stalks celery
    1 small red cabbage (~3 cups)
    1 small green cabbage (~3 cups)
    1 head romaine lettuce
    1 cup dulse sea vegetable
    1 cup water
    3 scallions, minced

1. Using scissors, cut dulse into small pieces.

2. Chop vegetables into long thin slices.

3. Mix dulse and vegetables thoroughly.

4. Press in a large bowl. A ceramic bowl with steep edges works best. Place a plate on top, one that is just slightly smaller than the diameter of the bowl. Place a weight on top. A glass gallon jug full of water works great, or another bowl or pot of water that fits inside the edges of the pressing bowl will work. Press for 4 or more hours.

5. Fold in dressing.

Lemon Tahini Dressing

½ cup sesame tahini

Juice of 2 lemons

½ cup water

¼ bunch fresh parsley, chopped fine, (~⅓ cup)

1. Combine ingredients, except parsley, and mix until smooth.

2. Mix in parsley.

Orange Baked Butternut Squash

PREP NOTES: When buying butternut squash, look for an intensely tan squash. Stripes of green skin mean it's not yet ripe. Other sweet winter squashes, such as buttercup, sweet mama, or kabocha squash would work just as wonderfully. The larger chunks add depth of texture to the dish. A large hotel pan is needed, preferably 20 by 12 by 2½ inches, or its equivalent. *See photo on page 192.*

> 3 medium butternut squashes
> 4 oranges
> 2 teaspoons cinnamon
> Pinch of sea salt

1. Peel squash, slice in half and remove seeds. Cut into square 2-inch chunks. (Approximate is fine.)

2. Remove zest from the oranges. Set aside. Squeeze juice from all the oranges (~1 cup).

3. Mix juice, zest, cinnamon and salt with squash.

4. Bake at 350 degrees in a covered baking pan for 1 hour, stirring the liquid and squash occasionally. Use baking sheets or foil to cover.

5. Check for moisture. If dry, add ¼ cup water. Continue baking until soft, but not mushy, for at least another 30 minutes.

Glazed Sautéed Carrots and Beets

PREP NOTES: The beets contrast with the orange color of the carrots, creating a beautiful dish. In general, when sautéing with water, always have a cup of water nearby and keep adding small amounts as the water evaporates.

> 2 or 3 large beets (~4 cups)
> 12 large carrots (~8 cups)
> 1 tablespoon olive oil *(optional)*
> 2 tablespoons brown rice vinegar
> 2 tablespoons brown rice syrup
> ½ teaspoon sea salt

1. Peel the beets, slice and cut into large slivers.

2. Peel the carrots, slice into large slivers.

3. In a covered large pan, sauté beets on medium heat in ½ tablespoon olive oil (or water) until almost tender, and then remove from pan.

4. In the same pan, sauté carrots in ½ tablespoon of olive oil (or water) until almost tender.

5. Stir in brown rice syrup, vinegar and salt with carrots and cook uncovered for a few minutes.

6. Gently mix in beets and simmer a few more minutes longer.

Pear Crisp with Vanilla Sauce

PREP NOTES: This crisp is also very tasty with 2 or 3 cups of fresh raspberries tossed in. Brown rice syrup, maple syrup, and nutmeg are used in multiple parts of this recipe. As a substitute for the maple sugar in the topping, increase the brown rice flour by ½ cup, and maple syrup by ¼ cup. A 12 by 20 by 2½ inch hotel pan, or the equivalent, is needed. A baking sheet or aluminum foil works fine for a cover.

Filling

1 cup dried pears

2 cups pear juice

14 to 16 large pears (Bosc or Bartlett)

1 cup brown rice syrup

Pinch of nutmeg

Pinch of sea salt

3 tablespoons arrowroot dissolved in ½ cup of the pear juice

1. Soak dried pears in 1½ cups pear juice for 10 minutes.

2. Remove the pears from the juice, setting the juice aside.

3. Chop dried pears into small ¼ inch pieces.

4. Peel, core and slice fresh pears into long thin wedges.

5. In baking pan, mix sliced pears, juice saved from soaking pears, chopped pears, brown rice syrup, nutmeg and sea salt.

6. Bake 15 minutes at 350 degrees.

7. Remove from heat and fold in arrowroot mixture.

Topping

1½ cups raw walnuts

5 cups gluten-free or regular rolled oats

2 cups brown rice flour

1 teaspoon sea salt

Pinch of cloves

½ teaspoon dried ginger

½ teaspoon nutmeg

½ cup maple sugar *(see Prep Notes for substitution)*

1 cup brown rice syrup

¾ cup applesauce, unsweetened

½ cup pure maple syrup

1 tablespoon vanilla

1. Toast walnuts in pan on stovetop, or in oven, until fragrant. Be mindful not to let walnuts burn. Chop coarsely. Set aside.

2. In a large bowl, mix together oats, rice flour, sea salt, walnuts, spices and maple sugar.

3. Whisk rice syrup, applesauce, maple syrup and vanilla together.

4. Pour wet ingredients into dry and mix thoroughly.

5. Crumble oat topping mixture over baked pears.

6. Bake at 350 degrees, covered for 40 minutes.

7. Uncover and bake 20 minutes more.

Vanilla Sauce

1 quart unsweetened vanilla soymilk
1 cup brown rice syrup
¼ cup pure maple syrup
2 vanilla beans (or 2 teaspoons vanilla extract)
Pinch of sea salt
6 tablespoons kuzu (or 4 tablespoons arrowroot)
6 tablespoons of water

1. Slice vanilla beans in half and place in small pot with soymilk.

2. Add all ingredients except kuzu and water.

3. Bring to slightly less than a boil, reduce heat and simmer for 15 minutes.

4. Strain out the pods of vanilla.

5. Thoroughly dissolve kuzu in 6 tablespoons of water and add to pot. Stir until the texture changes and the cloudiness clears. Turn off heat. Do not boil.

6. Drizzle sauce on pear crisp when serving.

A full plate from the May menu, see pages 91-105. A recipe for Kukicha Twig Tea is on page 225.

The Apprentice's Guide

By Alicia Freedman

OUR EXPERIENCE OF TASTE IS DEEPLY ROOTED IN the aesthetics of presentation. Inside Lewis and Priscilla's kitchen, the arrangement and shape of each chopped vegetable on a plate is carefully considered. Ideally, the finished product is a reflection of divine perfection. Every bite of food, prepared with love, holds an untold story within. It is a story of worship, respect and understanding. The community of friends, old and new, gathered together around the table can taste this in the food. They can feel it.

Wisdom rises in the steam pouring forth from pans, filling the room with a tantalizing aroma. The warmth expands and envelops contented diners with nourishment. For Lewis and Priscilla, working with food is a gratifying and stimulating endeavor and preparing healthy wholesome meals is a spiritual practice.

This section is meant to provide guidelines for incorporating macrobiotic principles into the kitchen. It also provides a practical list of utensils and ingredients that we consider essential.

We will begin by recommending that you use these ten less-common ingredients in your kitchen: sea salt, umeboshi plum vinegar, umeboshi plum paste, brown rice syrup, unhulled brown sesame seeds, sesame tahini, dark brown rice miso, light sweet white miso, agar-agar flakes and kuzu.

(right) *Priscilla and Alicia.*

A Guide to...

Working with Vegetables

Great wisdom is manifested in nature's design of each vegetable. Miraculous symmetry and balance are revealed to those who observe the shapes and textures of a seemingly ordinary vegetable. The concave circles of an onion, or the elongated crispness of a sturdy root vegetable express formations that are energetically aligned as expressions of life energy.

Mindfulness in food preparation enhances the experience of cooking. Vegetables are cut in a manner that honors the wisdom inherent in the plant's design, and this is why as much of the plant as possible is used. For instance, broccoli stalks are skinned and the core chopped rather than being discarded. Intuitively, a chef might also elect to serve green beans whole or save stock water to later be added back into a recipe. This type of preparation takes special attentiveness, since the more fibrous, yet edible, parts of plants often have different cooking times.

Size Cuts Used in This Book

- **minced** (tiny)

- **diced small** (¼ inch cubes, pea sized)

- **diced** (½ inch cubes)

- **chopped coarsely** (½ to ¾ inch pieces)

- **bite-sized** (sizes vary based on the vegetable's shape, but generally 1 to 2 square inches)

- **chunks** (approximately 2 inch square pieces)

To Peel or Not to Peel?

There is no need to peel most vegetables. We prefer to purchase organic produce and take advantage of the wealth of nutrients in the outer skins. Sometimes we peel carrots to make the color of a particular dish more vibrant, such as in blended carrot soup.

Cooking Styles Used in This Book

● **Baking:** A deeply warming and convenient way to cook vegetables, especially root vegetables and squashes in the winter months.

● **Blanching:** Briefly cook vegetables for two to five minutes in boiling water, and then remove with a large slotted spoon or long wooden handled wire mesh strainer. Immediately submerge vegetables in cold water to stop the cooking action, unless eaten immediately. Vegetables can become overcooked even after they are taken out of the heat. The objective is to cook the vegetable until the heat has permeated the center, but not much longer.

● **Boiling vegetables:** Vegetables can be cooked in boiling water until just done, retaining their bright color. Unlike blanched vegetables, boiled vegetables are not submerged in cold water immediately after cooking.

● **Pressing raw vegetables:** These crisp, raw and easily digested vegetable salads are the center of a balanced plate of food. Strips of vegetables, such as lettuce, cabbage, carrots, radishes, and celery are cut very thin. This exposes more surface area for the sea salt to draw water out through the cellular walls, thus breaking down the vegetables into a more digestible state. Mix salt into the thinly cut vegetables with your hands and press vegetables in a deep ceramic bowl with a plate that is slightly smaller than the opening of the bowl. This way the plate can slowly drop down as the vegetables are being pressed. We place a gallon jug full of water as the weight on the top. Water is released from the vegetables. After pressing for at least four hours, pour the accumulated water off, gently rinse the salt from the vegetables, and drain the rinse water out. *See photo page 69.*

● **Slow simmer:** A style of steaming and simmering vegetables with a little water and no oil. Start by bringing a little water and the vegetables to a boil and then quickly turning the heat down, allowing the vegetables to slowly cook until soft.

● **Steaming:** Vegetables are cooked with steam rather than by direct water contact. This can be done in a two-tiered steaming pot, or a multi-tiered bamboo steamer on a wok or large pot. Use enough water so that not all of it evaporates, but still does not touch the vegetables.

● **Water sautéing:** Instead of sautéing with oil, it is possible to cook vegetables in one or two tablespoons of water. As the water evaporates, continue to add a little more water, stirring to keep vegetables from sticking to the pan.

Sea Vegetables

All sea vegetables contain minerals, and are extremely helpful for acid-alkaline balance. Most sea vegetables need to be soaked before using. We sometimes share this soaking water with our houseplants, and other times it can be used in sauces and broths.

● **Agar-agar:** See the section on *Thickeners.*

● **Alaria:** Long, skinny and brownish in appearance. Soak for 15 minutes and cook for 10 to 15 minutes. Used in soups, it is especially good

in miso soup. This Atlantic Ocean crop is harvested in the US. It is a little tougher than its Japanese sister wakame, because it has not been blanched prior to drying.

- **Arame:** Consists of little black curly pieces. Soak for 30 minutes, and then cook for 15 to 20 minutes. Arame has a mild semi-sweet flavor and is an excellent source of many trace minerals.

- **Dulse:** Reddish in color. This fabulous sea vegetable can be dry-roasted in a pan or toasted in the oven, and can also be sprinkled as a garnish for soups. It makes a great condiment when combined with seeds, especially sunflower and pumpkin. We also like it raw in pressed salads. It is delicious on oatmeal.

- **Hiziki:** (sometimes spelled Hijiki) Wiry black sticks which are a little thicker than arame. Soak for at least 30 minutes, and then cook for 30 to 45 minutes. Use in salads or cooked vegetable dishes. It goes well with onions, scallions and corn. Protein-rich foods such as crumbled tofu, edamame, tempeh, peanut sauce and tahini, draw the intense flavor out. Full of nutrients, it is very potent and best eaten in small amounts.

- **Kelp:** Flat, wide and thick. The complex sugars, high mineral content and naturally occuring glutomic acid helps beans taste great and digest easily.

- **Kombu:** Flat, wide and thick, similar to kelp. It softens and breaks down when cooked with beans, and in the process tenderizes and makes the beans more digestible.

- **Nori:** This tasty sea vegetable can be eaten on its own. Do not soak nori as it falls apart when wet. It is usually sold toasted in square flat sheets. If it is untoasted, simply toast it briefly over a medium flame on the stove. Used primarily for sushi.

- **Wakame:** Thin, long and green in appearance. It is served in salads, healing miso soup and vegetable dishes.

Beans / Legumes

- **All beans** (except lentils and split peas) need to be pre-soaked to soften them for quicker cooking. Soaking also converts the indigestible starches in the bean's outer membrane to a more digestible form. Always give enough time to fully cook the beans, as you may have problems digesting them otherwise. It is not necessary to eat a large amount of beans to be well-nourished. When first adding beans to your diet, eat small quantities, allowing your digestive enzymes to build up. Different combinations of spices, herbs, and vegetables also assist with bean digestion. Cooked beans will last for days in the refrigerator, ready to be added to soup or another dish.

- **Tempeh:** A very satisfying whole, cultured soybean food with a distinctive taste. Thorough cooking makes tempeh more appealing.

- **Tofu:** This soybean food can take on many different personalities, as it easily incorporates other flavors. It is used for desserts, sauces, or as a main dish. It is wholesome, but, technically not a whole food. It is made from soymilk instead of directly from the bean. We always have it in the refrigerator as it can be easily and conveniently used for a quick meal. Kids love it.

yellow
split pea

kidney

green
split pea

red lentil

black

chick peas

navy

green lentil

red chili

millet

rolled oats

long-grain
brown rice

quinoa

corn grits

kasha

short-grain
brown rice

Grains

Certain grains have qualities that suit different seasons. Here are the grains we use in this cookbook:

- **Oats** are naturally gluten-free. However, they are often contaminated from gluten-containing grains when harvested, stored or processed. If on a gluten-free diet, purchase gluten-free oats that are protected from this cross-contamination. Oats are great for making creamy soup bases and for crusts and toppings in desserts.

- **Kasha** is also known as buckwheat groats. Kasha is a warming winter grain from the rhubarb family. Croquettes are a wonderful way to enjoy kasha.

- **Basmati brown rice** has a fragrant aroma and is delicious when combined with fresh sweet corn kernels. We make a wonderful rice pudding with it.

- **Long grain brown rice** has cooling properties and is, therefore, mainly eaten in the summer. Like all brown rice, it is minimally processed and so retains its nutrients.

- **Short grain brown rice** has warming properties, especially when pressure-cooked. It is a main staple of the macrobiotic diet, as it is very balanced and nutritious. It is a great source of strength, energy and endurance.

- **Corn** is used as a grain when it has been dried and ground. Corn meal is more finely ground than grits. We use corn grits in polenta and corn meal in muffins.

- **Millet** was Leonardo DaVinci's favorite grain and is known as the "queen of grains". It is relatively new to the United States, but is common in Africa. It is the most alkalizing grain, easy to digest, and has a mild, sweet, nutty flavor.

- **Quinoa** is a complete protein. This beautiful, tightly curled small grain cooks fast. It is a wonderful gluten-free substitute for wheat tabouli.

Salt and Savory

- **Sea salt:** Contains a vast array of trace minerals as it is harvested from evaporated seawater. Switching from processed table salt to sea salt is the first change we recommend when transitioning to a healthier diet.

- **Wheat-free tamari:** Made from fermented soy. We always use wheat-free tamari to accommodate gluten-free diets. Shoyu and soy sauce are often not wheat-free.

- **Umeboshi plums and paste:** Made from pickled Japanese ume plums. We use these in salad dressings and nori rolls, which adds a distinctly pungent flavor. It balances the blood and is helpful when you have eaten too many sweets.

- **Miso:** Sold in the refrigerator section. There are many kinds, but we will focus on two varieties here. Brown rice miso: Savory and naturally fermented for about two years. When using in soup, add after reducing to a simmer at the end of cooking. Boiling miso destroys the enzymes, and thus the healing properties. Sweet white miso: Also called mellow miso, it is cured for less time than the dark miso and has a lighter and sweeter taste. It is used in sweet vegetable soups, with corn, for example. The lighter miso is used in dressings, sauces and other raw dishes.

Optional Oils

The oils we use sparingly are sesame and toasted sesame oil, olive and safflower oil. We use sesame or olive oil for sautéing. They have a stronger flavor and are thick enough to sauté properly. Sesame oil is very stable. Safflower is better for baking because it is thin and has a lighter flavor. Toasted sesame oil is rich and tasty in stir-fries and other sautéed dishes.

We have included oil-free options in the recipes. For oil-free sautéing, simply omit the oil and use water instead. For other dishes, substitute a nut or seed to create a rich flavor.

mirin   **brown rice vinegar**   **umeboshi plum vinegar**   **balsamic vinegar**

Vinegars

- **Mirin:** Rice cooking wine that is made from sweet rice. It is maltier and sweeter than plain rice vinegar.

- **Brown rice vinegar:** Has minerals that white rice vinegar does not offer and is more of a whole food. The taste is sharper than umeboshi plum vinegar.

- **Umeboshi plum vinegar:** Has a salty, pungent and sour stand-alone flavor. It is so unique that we often use it as the only addition to cooked greens.

- **Balsamic vinegar:** This vinegar has a complete flavor. It is made from grapes and has a tinge of sweetness.

Sweeteners

- **Brown rice syrup:** Trace minerals and complex carbohydrates make this a more whole and complete food than refined or raw sugar. The long chains of sugar in brown rice syrup are released into the blood stream more evenly than many other sweeteners. It is a substantial, grounding source of rich sweetness.

- **Pure fruit juice:** Orange, pear, cherry and apple juices are used to reconstitute dried fruit, sweeten desserts and enliven dressings and sauces. Select 100% juice with nothing added.

- **Pure maple syrup:** Maple syrup and maple sugar are used for the rich and smoky maple taste. Select 100% pure maple syrup.

Thickeners

- **Agar-agar (kanten):** Traditionally made by freezing and drying extracts of various red sea vegetables. It is sold as flakes, powder or a bar. When cooked, it has the consistency of gelatin, with no discernible flavor. Most often, we use the flakes, which are less processed and more consistent than the powder form. Flakes do not clump up the way that powder can.

- **Arrowroot:** Extracted from the dried root of a large perennial. When using, first dissolve in cold water or other liquids.

- **Kuzu (or Kudzu):** Made from the dried root of the Kudzu plant, which grows wild in the Southeastern United States. When using, first dissolve in cold water. It is very mild and takes on the flavor of any sauce or gravy. Aids in digestion.

Useful Cooking Conversions

- 3 teaspoons = 1 tablespoon
- 2 tablespoons = 1 ounce
- 8 ounces = 1 cup
- 2 cups = 1 pint
- 2 pints = 1 quart
- 4 quarts = 1 gallon

Scaling Down Recipes for Smaller Quantities

The recipes in this book are all designed for 20-24 portions, unless stated otherwise. These will all convert (scale) very easily and reliably to smaller quantities.

A clear and easy way to do this would be to make a simple chart to calculate the reduced amount of each ingredient.

Here is an illustration for the first recipe in this book, **Green Split Pea and Navy Bean Soup** *(page 30)*.

Ingredient	to serve 20-24 *(as written)*	to serve 10-12 *(divide by 2)*	to serve 5-6 *(divide by 4)*
Navy Beans	2 cups	1 cup	½ cup
Green Split Peas	4 cups	2 cups	1 cup
Kombu	1 four-inch strip	1 two-inch strip	1 one-inch strip
Water	12 cups	6 cups	3 cups
Carrots	6 med. (3 cups)	3 med. (1½ cups)	1 large (¾ cup)
Yellow Onions	2 med. (~2½ cups)	1 med. (~1¼ cups)	½ med. (½ - ¾ cup)
Red Onions	2 med. (~2½ cups)	1 med. (~¼ cups)	½ med. (½ - ¾ cup)
Sea salt	1 teaspoon	½ teaspoon	¼ teaspoon
Celery stalks	8 stalks	4 stalks	2 stalks
Tamari	4 tablespoons	2 tablespoons	1 tablespoon
Parsley	1 bunch	½ bunch	¼ bunch

Tools

- Hotel pans come in different depths, but the standard size is 12 by 20 by 2½ inches.

- A suribachi is a ceramic bowl with ridges, used with a wooden pestle, called a surikogi, to grind dulse (a sea vegetable), gomashio (roasted sesame seeds and salt) and other condiments.

- 20 to 24 small bowls for desserts

- Glass gallon jug or other suitable weight for presses

- 5-liter pressure cooker

- Long wooden handled wire strainer for scooping vegetables out of boiling water

- Food processer or high-quality blender

- Whisk

- Knives: small paring knife, 8-10 inch French or chef's knife, 6½ inch Japanese vegetable knife

- Two-tiered bamboo steamer or metal steaming pot

- Zester (A grater works, but a zester is the better tool for the job.)

- Small ceramic Japanese ginger grater

- Bamboo sushi mat

- Large cast iron frying pan with lid. A 12 inch diameter by 2 inch deep pan works well for large portions

- 10-inch springform pan, for the Almond Un-Cheesecake.

- Large metal bowls for mixing

- Large heavy bottomed pot, 8 quarts with lid

In terms of materials, we consider how the food will interact with the containers it is cooked in, taking into account what is practical and what is attractive. We prefer quality stainless steel for most of our mixing bowls, pots and pans. Cast iron pans are also essential. Ceramic and glass are great materials for bowls, but break easily.

suribachi

.rikogi

mesh strainer

wire
strainer

japanese
vegetable
knife

whisk

paring
knife

ginger
grater

chef's
knife

zester

Set Up Wisdom

- Have the necessary tools needed before starting to cook, such as enough mixing bowls, trays, pots and pans. If you are new at this, make a list of materials along with the ingredients.

- Figure out the order for what's going to happen on the burners and inside the oven. We make desserts the day before we serve dinner. Cold dishes, such as pressed and green salads, can be made early in the day. Leave more than enough time for the beans to cook. Ideally, it is best to chop everything first and then cook all the dishes as close to serving time as possible. First, make the foods that can be cooked and then warmed in the oven until serving. We always boil greens last because they cook and cool down quickly, and are usually served hot.

- Do not use hot water from the tap for consumption. Hot tap water may contain contaminants from the hot water heater and water pipes. It is better to draw cold water from the tap and heat it on the stove.

- If the bottom of a thick soup is burning, turn off the heat. Do not stir. Let it sit for a few minutes. If it has just started to burn, the bottom can be loosened and stirred in and then you can continue cooking at a lower heat. If the bottom is badly burned, then transfer it to another pot without disturbing the bottom.

- Here are some ways to taste samples without breaking the rules of safe preparation. Drip tastes from a big stirring spoon onto a small tasting spoon. To taste the impact of a possible modification before adding it to the whole dish, put a small amount of the food in a tea cup and add seasoning to this small amount first.

- Washing dishes can be the most important job in the kitchen. Start cooking in a clean kitchen and wash dishes while you cook to keep the space workable. Ideally it is best to have the dishes done, dried and put away when guests arrive.

Kukicha Twig Tea

We always have Kukicha Twig Tea available for our guests. Kukicha means "twig tea" in Japanese. This tea is the actual twigs of the traditional tea plant. These twigs are dry roasted and sold in bulk or in bags. The tea has a very small amount of caffeine, only a few milligrams per cup, as opposed to 75 milligrams in a cup of black tea and 150 in coffee. Kukicha tea's alkalizing properties create a rich, balanced beverage.

Serve hot or cold. Kukicha makes delicious iced tea when simmered with some fresh mint and then cooled. Also, it is great cold, mixed with a small amount of apple juice. The twigs can be reused once or twice.

> **5 quarts water**
> **1 cup dried Kukicha Twigs**

1. Bring water to a boil, reduce to low, add twigs. Cover and simmer for at least 1 hour. Two or three hours is even better.

We are forever grateful to Alicia, Julie and Theresa for their significant contributions to this book.

● **Alicia Freedman:** Lucky for us, since early in life, Alicia embraced the art of photography and has now shared this gift with us. Additionally, Alicia's ability to put herself in the beginner's mind allowed the apprentice section to manifest as a wonderful guide.

● **Julie Manners:** A graphic designer by trade, Julie created the beautiful layout and design of this book. Julie has the patience of a saint for being so graciously accommodating to our constant revisions.

● **Theresa Joseph:** As well as being an amazing gardener, Theresa shared some of her other talents with us by editing and testing many of the recipes. Theresa, and her partner Russ Cornwell, have stepped up to the plate and hosted our weekly dinner on occasion when we have traveled out of town.

A few more words about us…

● **Priscilla Timberlake:** As a mother of four, she has spent a lot of time in the kitchen. Priscilla enjoys teaching cooking classes at home and at our local cooperative market. She also teaches personal growth and wellness classes at Cornell University. Priscilla loves connecting with students from all over the world.

● **Lewis Freedman:** In addition to being a dad, and a nutritionist, he also teaches yoga and stress management classes at Cornell University. As an instructor in the online Certificate in Plant-Based Nutrition program by eCornell and the T. Colin Campbell Foundation, Lewis is directly involved with the growing global movement toward embracing a whole food, plant-based diet.

(l-r) *Alicia, Julie, Priscilla, Lewis and Theresa*

ACKNOWLEDGEMENTS

OUR PARENTS

⬤ **Jean Timberlake,** for her openness to new possibilities. **Joe Timberlake,** for embracing the joy of cooking. **Carole Freedman** for her commitment to providing delicious meals for her family. **Gary Freedman** for his sense of humor and love of food.

OUR SIBLINGS

⬤ For always being there: **Amanda,** her husband **Ed**, **Tim**, his wife **Evie, Abigail, Randi, Cindy,** her husband **Ron** and **Sara**.

OUR CHILDREN

⬤ For giving us honest feedback over the years: **Jonah**, his wife **Alicia, Tyler, Arden** and **Raina**.

DEDICATED RECIPE TESTERS

⬤ **Lydia Albonesi, Deborah Berman, Lan Berman, Russ Cornwell, Anita Devine, Alicia Freedman, Jonah Freedman, Susie Gutierrez, Theresa Joseph, Harmony Keeley Young, Karen Keeley, Julie Manners, Isaac Spencer, Raina Timberlake-Freedman, Bill White** and **Lisa White**.

PRISCILLA'S COOKING MENTORS

⬤ **Aveline Kushi,** for sharing her wisdom in my first cooking class. **Mark Kelso,** a former chef at Kripalu Center for Yoga & Health, for offering his friendly guidance. **Judy Genova,** who enthusiastically taught macrobiotic cooking classes and opened the door for me to the world of sea vegetables. **Peggy Aker,** owner of Macro Mamas, in Ithaca, NY, for being an example of a master chef in action!

EDITORS

⬤ **Theresa Joseph, Alicia Freedman and Mary Pernal** read and edited this book cover to cover.

PRINTER LIAISON

⬤ **Della Mancuso** coordinated the printing of this book and made the extra effort to acquire the finest quality 100% recycled paper.

SUPPLIERS

⬤ **Erick Smith** of Cayuga Pure Organics grows a variety of beans and grains just minutes from our doorstep. www.cporganics.com

⬤ **Theresa Joseph,** our dear friend and neighborhood farmer, blesses us with fresh, organic produce.

⬤ **Larch Hanson** has been harvesting nutritious sea vegetables off the coast of Maine for decades. www.theseaweedman.com

⬤ **GreenStar Natural Foods Market** is our local co-op, whose ongoing service to the Ithaca, NY community deserves extra-special recognition! www.greenstar.coop

⬤ **Natural Import Company** of Ashville, NC has been supplying us with high-quality macrobiotic ingredients for years. www.naturalimport.com

⬤ **Suzanne's Specialties** offers organic brown rice syrup, which we use in every dessert in this book! www.suzannes-specialties.com

(l-r) *Erick Smith, Theresa Joseph and Larch Hanson*

...We Especially Wish to Thank Everyone...

INDEX